Rubber Stamped Jewelry

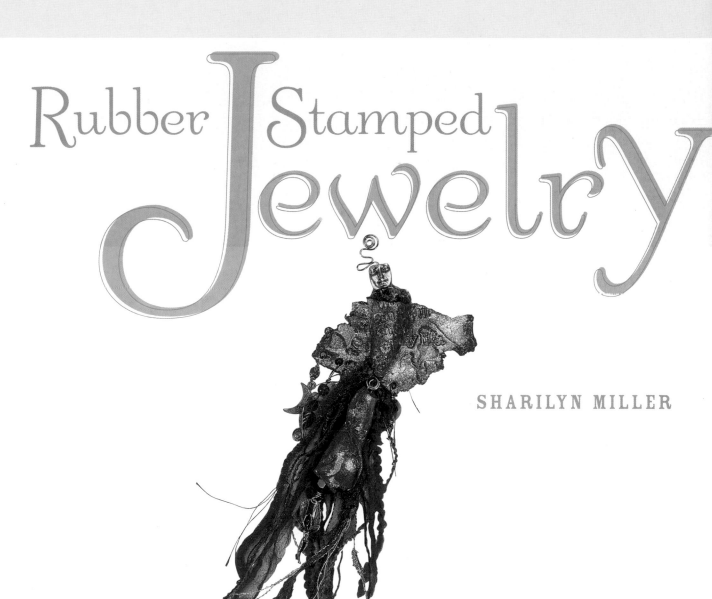

SHARILYN MILLER

NORTH LIGHT BOOKS
Cincinnati, Ohio

www.artistsnetwork.com

I would like to **DEDICATE** *this book to three very special friends: Louise Duhamel, Joyce Boyd-Wells and Anne Reiss. Jewelry designers all three, they have inspired me with their artistry, creativity, and most important of all, their generosity of spirit. To the gals in Louise's kitchen!*

METRIC CONVERSION CHART

TO CONVERT	TO	MULTIPLY BY
Inches	Centimeters	2.54
Centimeters	Inches	0.4
Feet	Centimeters	30.5
Centimeters	Feet	0.03
Yards	Meters	0.9
Meters	Yards	1.1
Sq. Inches	Sq. Centimeters	6.45
Sq. Centimeters	Sq. Inches	0.16
Sq. Feet	Sq. Meters	0.09
Sq. Meters	Sq. Feet	10.8
Sq. Yards	Sq. Meters	0.8
Sq. Meters	Sq. Yards	1.2
Pounds	Kilograms	0.45
Kilograms	Pounds	2.2
Ounces	Grams	28.4
Grams	Ounces	0.04

07 06 05 04   5 4 3 2

Library of Congress Cataloging-in-Publication Data

Miller, Sharilyn.
   Rubber stamped jewelry / Sharilyn Miller.-- 1st ed.
      p. cm.
   ISBN 1-58180-384-2 (pbk. : alk. paper)
   1. Jewelry making. 2. Rubber stamp printing. 3. Wire craft. I. Title.
   TT212.M53 2003
   745.594'2--dc21
                           2003043636

EDITORS: Liz Schneiders and Krista Hamilton
DESIGNER: Andrea Short
LAYOUT ARTIST: Karla Baker
PRODUCTION COORDINATOR: Michelle Ruberg
PHOTOGRAPHERS: Christine Polomsky and Al Parrish
PHOTO STYLIST: Jan Nickum

SHARILYN MILLER is the author of *Stamp Art* (1999) and *The Stamp Artist's Project Book* (2001) published by Rockport Publishers. She is Editor-in-Chief of three magazines published by Stampington & Company: *Somerset Studio*, a publication for art stampers, papercrafter and lettering artists; *Belle Armoire*, an art-to-wear magazine featuring handmade garments, jewelry and fashion accessories; and *Art Doll Quarterly*.

Sharilyn became the editor of *Somerset Studio* shortly before it was launched in January 1997. She launched *Belle Armoire* on April 1, 2001 and *Art Doll Quarterly* on May 1, 2003. Prior to working in the craft magazine industry, she was a reporter with *The Orange County Register* in Santa Ana, California. She holds a commercial art degree from the Northwest College of Art, Poulsbo, Washington, and a degree in print journalism communications from the California State University, Fullerton.

VISIT SHARILYN'S WEB SITE AT :

www.SharilynMiller.com

ACKNOWLEDGMENTS...

Writing a book is an adventure, especially when so many creative, talented and generous people are involved in the project. My small part as author is only one cog in a giant wheel of skill, creativity and earnest effort that came together in this project. The many artists who contributed their jewelry designs, the photographers, designers, editors and the production staff all made invaluable contributions. *Rubber Stamped Jewelry* is in every way a collaborative effort, and I owe a huge debt of gratitude to everyone who participated in its creation.

First, I must thank the talented stamp artists who contributed their innovative rubber stamped jewelry designs, instructions and support. You will find their names listed in the table of contents. Obviously this book would not exist without their generous contributions, and I will always be their number-one fan!

Next I must thank my editors, Liz Schneiders and Krista Hamilton, who helped shepherd this book along—not an easy task! I thoroughly enjoyed working with Liz and photographer Christine Polomsky during our week-long photo shoot in Cincinnati, Ohio, in the summer of 2002. We worked hard but had so many laughs throughout that I felt our time together was much too short. It's nice to be able to count your coworkers as friends.

Special thanks are also due to acquisitions editor Tricia Waddell, who bravely took a chance on a book of rubber stamped jewelry design—which has never been done before now. Thank you for believing in my vision, Tricia! And while I never had the pleasure of meeting the book designer, Andrea Short, I think it's obvious how important her contribution was to this project.

THANK YOU, everyone, for making this book a reality. Creating it was an adventure; your contributions turned a dream into the reality you now hold in your hands.

TABLE OF CONTENTS

PROJECT GALLERY

page **54**

left to right: Tag Art {PAGE 60} · An Eye for an Ear...or a Neck {PAGE 72} · Renaissance Impressions {PAGE 74} · Buddha's Delight {PAGE 102}

STAMP MAINTENANCE

With proper care, your stamps will last many years. Sunlight, however, can dry out the rubber and render it incapable of absorbing ink. Always store your rubber stamps in a dark place.

To prolong their wear, clean your stamps after each use with a commercial stamp cleaner. Or, moisten a paper towel with a weak mixture of water and household window cleaner, and pat your stamp onto the paper towel to remove the ink. Some stamp pros use commercial baby wipes to clean their stamps. This is not only gentle to the rubber, but the moisturizers help to keep it supple.

When using unmounted stamps and acrylic paints, allow the stamps to soak in water during your stamp session. When finished, remove the stamps and scrub them under running water with an old toothbrush. Never submerse mounted stamps in water. This may loosen the glue that holds the rubber and cushion to the wood.

APPLY AN EVEN COAT
Dab the rubber stamp onto the inkpad for an even application.

CREATING A GOOD IMPRESSION

Stamping is a fun and easy way to embellish jewelry, but there are some things to keep in mind that will help you create professional-looking images.

Begin by selecting a stamp. Ink the rubber image evenly, and press the stamp firmly onto the print surface. Don't rock the stamp as you press it down. This will make the edges blur or smudge. Lift the stamp away quickly, holding down the print surface to prevent liftoff.

When stamping with fabric paints or acrylics, pour a small amount of paint onto a disposable palette such as a Styrofoam plate or a sheet of freezer paper. Tap a soft sponge into the paint, dab most of the pigment onto a paper towel, and sponge it on the stamp. Stamp immediately, and either reapply paint to make another impression, or clean the stamp right away to keep the paint from drying permanently onto the rubber.

Sometimes a rubber stamp is used without pigment to press an image into a soft surface such as clay. In this case, you may ink the stamp beforehand. If you ink a stamp with pigment ink before stamping into clay, the ink will be permanently bonded to the surface once the clay has been cured.

PRESS DOWN FIRMLY
Press the stamp down firmly to avoid smudging.

INK LARGE STAMPS FACE-UP
Ink large rubber stamps by placing them face-up on a hard surface and applying the inkpad to the stamp itself.

COLORING A STAMPED IMAGE

There are many options for coloring stamped images. Feel free to experiment with a variety of media, including chalk, ink, paint, colored pencils, metallic rub-ons and more.

DECORATE THE PAPER
Decorate your paper with color before stamping your image.

DECORATE THE STAMPED IMAGE
Once you have stamped an image, decorate it with the art medium of your preference.

STAMP THE IMAGE
Press the stamp firmly on the decorated paper.

USE A SPONGE APPLICATOR
Sponge applicator tips in a variety of shapes can be used to stamp repeat background patterns.

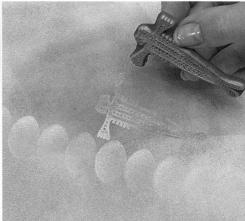

EXPERIMENT WITH COLOR
To create an interesting stamped image, apply small amounts of different colored inks to the stamp. The result will be a colorful surprise!

HEAT EMBOSSING

Heat embossing is a technique used to raise an image above the printing surface. This requires an embossing agent—usually powder—which is heated with an embossing tool that blows very hot air out of a pointed nozzle.

To emboss, stamp your image onto the surface with pigment ink. Sprinkle embossing powder over the inked image to cover it completely while the ink is still damp. Shake off the excess powder. Allow your embossing tool to heat up, and then hold the nozzle a few inches above the image until the powder melts. When finished, your stamped image will have a raised, dimensional surface.

POLYMER CLAY
EMBELLISHMENTS

Polymer clay is one of the most versatile craft mediums available to the modern artist. It's easy to work with, appropriate for all age groups (with adult supervision), available in a rainbow of hues, and can be used to make a wide variety of accessories, jewelry pieces and embellishments. Before you begin using polymer clay, there are a few things you should know.

 BASIC POLYMER CLAY MATERIALS

There are a few things you will need to purchase before beginning your polymer clay embellishments:

POLYMER CLAY: man-made clay that is soft and pliable and becomes permanently hard when baked in an oven; available in a wide variety of colors; popular brands include Sculpey, Fimo and Premo

ROLLING PIN

HAND-CRANKED PASTA MACHINE: pasta-making device used to condition, blend and roll clay into flat sheets of varying thickness

TISSUE BLADE: sharp, smooth, bendable blade used to slice thin layers of polymer clay

SANDING BLOCK: used wet for smoothing the surface of baked polymer clay

SCULPTING TOOLS: any hard, textured tool that may be used to create shapes or surface texture on polymer clay

BRAYER: see Basic Stamping Materials, page 30.

GOLD, SILVER, COPPER OR VARIEGATED LEAF: extremely thin sheet of real metal that can be applied to raw polymer clay prior to baking

POLYMER CLAY MATERIALS
(left to right) polymer clay, embossing powder, metal leaf

CLEAR EMBOSSING INK: thick, clear ink applied to rubber stamps to prevent them from sticking to raw clay

CLAY-DEDICATED TOASTER OVEN: used to bake clay, usually at 275°F (135°C), until it hardens (approximately 20 minutes)

OTHER INCLUSIONS: embossing powder, metallic rub-ons, chalks, beads

 CHOOSING AND STORING POLYMER CLAY

Polymer clay is marketed under many different brand names—Sculpey, Fimo and Premo, to name a few—and in a wide variety of colors. Choosing your clay can be a challenge.

My personal favorite is Premo because it is more malleable and is available in many beautiful metallic and pearlescent colors. Some artists prefer Fimo or Fimo Soft, which are stiffer in texture. Many clay artists start out with the economical Super Sculpey or Sculpey III. A new clay on the market called Kato Polyclay is also very good.

Experiment with small packets of different brands until you find the one that meets your needs. Polymer clay is sold in craft stores, art supply stores and online.

Always store polymer clay in its original package, wrapped in wax paper, and in a plastic container. Store the container away from direct sunlight, heat and dust. If left in the car on a hot day, clay will bake to rock hardness.

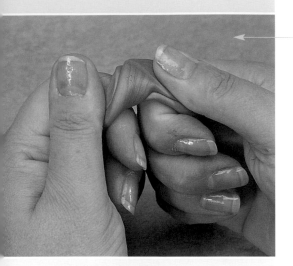

CONDITION THE CLAY
Roll your clay into a snake, double the snake and roll it again. Twist it, bend it and generally soften it before running it through a hand-cranked pasta machine.

SAFETY GUIDELINES

Polymer clay is nontoxic, so working with it shouldn't pose a problem for adults or supervised children. (It must not be ingested, of course.) The Art and Craft Materials Institute has certified the clay as nontoxic. It carries the ASTM D4236 designation, meaning that it can be handled safely by artists of all ages.

While working with raw polymer clay, avoid rubbing your eyes. Wash your hands frequently, especially before eating. Tools and equipment that come in contact with raw or baked polymer clay must never be used to prepare or serve food.

Always bake polymer clay in a room with excellent ventilation. Leave at least one window open. It's best to reserve a "dedicated oven" for baking polymer clay. Using your home oven is an option for infrequent baking, but you must thoroughly wash out the inside afterward with baking soda and water. Otherwise, the fumes will be re-released when you use the oven later.

CONDITIONING POLYMER CLAY

Polymer clay must be conditioned before use, but some types require more work than others. The purpose of conditioning the clay is twofold: to soften it and make it easier to work with, and to strengthen it and make it less likely to break after baking.

Fimo can be very hard and even crumbly, so it may have to be chopped up in a small food processor before running it through a hand-cranked pasta machine. Softer clay can be kneaded, rolled and manipulated like bread dough. To speed up the process, run it through a pasta machine about 20 times.

Should you accidentally over-condition your clay, making it too soft to work with, allow it to rest for 20 minutes in a cool, dry place.

BAKING POLYMER CLAY

Preheat your oven to 275°F (135°C). Once it has been preheated, place your finished pieces inside on a baking sheet lined with cardstock or matboard to prevent shiny spots from developing on the clay surface. When baking a large piece, it may be necessary to prop it up and drape a tent of aluminum foil over it to protect it from the heating element.

Bake clay beads on a skewer or place them on cotton balls to keep them from flattening. Always follow the manufacturer's instructions regarding baking times and temperatures. Most clay projects are baked at 275°F (135°C) for 20-25 minutes.

BUFFING, SANDING AND DRILLING BAKED POLYMER CLAY

Once baked, polymer clay may be wet-sanded to polish the surface. Sanding with progressively finer grades of sandpaper is the best way to produce a nice finish. Buffing tools may also be used. Some artists paint a water-based varnish on the surface as well. Baked clay can be drilled with an ordinary electric drill to create button and bead holes, or to dangle chains, fibers or charms.

ADDING METALLIC FLECKS TO POLYMER CLAY

There are numerous techniques with which to decorate your clay. One of my favorites is metal leafing, which adds a rich, metallic sheen to ordinary polymer clay.

② ADHERE THE LEAF TO THE CLAY
Run the clay through a hand-cranked pasta machine on a tight setting to press the leafing material into the clay. This will cause it to separate, creating a lovely surface design. The resulting clay may be used to make beads and pendants, or to cover large objects that may be incorporated into your jewelry.

① APPLY METALLIC LEAFING MATERIAL
To create clay sheets with lovely silver or gold leaf patterns, roll out a thin sheet of conditioned clay. Next, place the sheet onto a page of leafing material. This will stick to the clay.

STAMPING IN POLYMER CLAY

It is easy to add texture to polymer clay with rubber stamps and other materials. Once the clay is conditioned, it is soft enough to hold the impression. To prevent the clay from sticking, tap some clear embossing ink on the stamp. The ink acts as a release agent and will not show in the final result.

 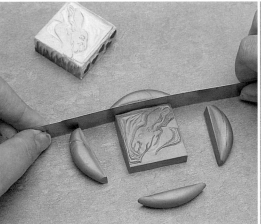 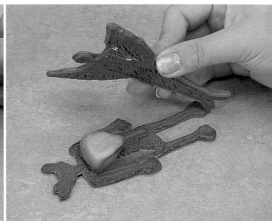

STAMP INTO THE CLAY
Use mounted or unmounted rubber stamps to create impressions in polymer clay.

TRIM THE STAMPED IMAGE
Once you have stamped your image, use a sharp tissue blade to remove excess clay.

MAKE A SANDWICH
To add texture to both sides, sandwich clay between two stamps.

CREATING MARBELED POLYMER CLAY

Another technique, marbeling, also requires the use of a hand-cranked pasta machine. Running the clay through the machine several times will not only blend two or more colors of clay, but it will condition the clay at the same time.

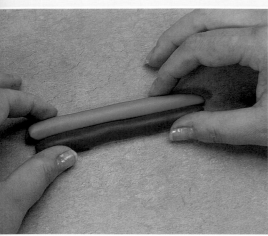

1 ROLL OUT THE CLAY
Start by rolling out two different colored logs of clay of equal length and thickness.

2 TWIST THE LOGS
Twist the logs together tightly as shown.

3 MELD THE COLORS
Run the twisted clay through a hand-cranked pasta machine on a wide setting.

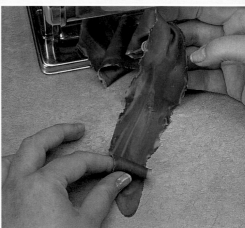

4 CONTINUE TO MARBLE THE CLAY
Tighten the setting on the pasta machine, and continue running the clay through until it is marbled to your satisfaction.

Applying Surface Color

There are several ways in which to embellish raw polymer clay, including metallic rub-ons, chalk, glitter and interference pigments

ADD HIGHLIGHTS
Before baking the clay, you may add highlights of color with metallic rub-ons.

APPLY DRY PIGMENTS
Polymer clay can be further embellished before baking by applying chalk, gold leaf and other craft materials with a soft brush.

EXPLORE YOUR OPTIONS
Interference pigments, which produce a glittering effect in matte and gloss finishes, may also be applied to raw clay. The pigments will bond to the clay during baking, but they will not stick when applied to baked clay unless they are first mixed with glue or varnish.

ANTIQUING POLYMER CLAY

Create the illusion of old beads and buttons with antiquing. This technique will not only make your brand new creations look like valuable antiques, but it is also great for hiding mistakes made along the way.

① PAINT THE CLAY

Once rubber stamped clay has been baked and allowed to cool, it can be painted with acrylics. One option is to create an "antiqued" appearance by rubbing the clay with black acrylic paint.

② WIPE AWAY EXCESS PAINT

While the paint is still wet, wipe away the excess with a rag. Allow the color of the clay to show through, leaving the black paint in the crevices.

③ APPLY THE DRY-BRUSH TECHNIQUE

To prepare to drybrush acrylic paint onto polymer clay, squeeze a few drops of paint onto a paper towel or painter's palette. Dip a flat brush into the paint, and brush most of the paint onto a towel until the brush is nearly dry.

④ PAINT THE HIGHLIGHTS

Gently whisk the tip of the paintbrush against the clay, catching the highlights of the stamped surface. Dip the brush into another paint color, brush off most of the color, and drybrush the clay again. Repeat this process to create multicolored clay.

CREATING POLYMER CLAY BEADS

Many types of beads can be made with polymer clay. It can be rolled out flat and shaped with mandrels, like the rollup bead and pinch bead, or it can be rolled into a ball, stamped and fashioned as a button.

1 CREATE SMALL ROLLUP BEADS
CUT OUT THE SHAPES

Cut rubber stamped clay into triangles. Flip a triangle over so that the patterned side is hidden, and lay a bamboo skewer against one edge of the triangle as shown.

2 ROLL UP THE BEAD

Holding the skewer against the clay, use your thumbs to pick up the edge of the clay and press it gently against the skewer. Roll the bead forward onto the skewer and gently press down the triangle tip.

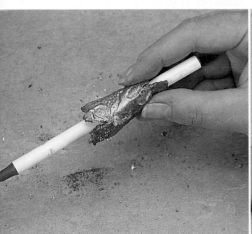 

CREATE LARGE ROLLUP BEADS

Wrap a torn piece of clay around a large mandrel such as a pen. Place the bead on soft cotton balls to keep it from flattening while it cures.

MAKE A PINCH BEAD

Cut or tear out a piece of rubber stamped clay. Push a large mandrel under the clay, and gently pinch it to create a form.

MAKE HOLES IN BEADS

Use a bamboo skewer to poke holes in your clay beads for buttons.

CREATING POLYMER CLAY BEAD MOLDS

It is easy to duplicate your favorite bead or button with polymer clay. Use a mold over and over again to create matching buttons, or simply create another one with scrap polymer clay.

1 MAKE AN IMPRESSION

Press your thumb into a large ball of polymer clay to create an indentation. Press the bead firmly into the indentation as shown.

2 REVEAL THE IMAGE

Remove the bead from the clay, and see if you like the impression you've made. If not, simply repeat the process until you have obtained the desired result. Bake as directed.

3 MAKE A BEAD FROM THE MOLD

Once the clay mold has cooled, condition a piece of polymer clay and roll it into a ball. Press the ball into the clay mold.

4 EXAMINE YOUR WORK

Remove the clay from the mold. You now have an impression identical to the original bead.

FIBER ART
EMBELLISHMENTS

Fibers such as thread, yarn, hemp and embroidery floss add a distinctive touch to handmade jewelry. Artists are experimenting more and more with different fibers, from metallic embroidery threads to boutique yarns in various colors and textures. Another alternative is silk ribbon, which may be crocheted, braided or knotted into beautiful jewelry. With a touch of imagination, you'll find lots of ways to incorporate these materials into wearable art.

 ## BASIC FIBER ART MATERIALS

Visit your local craft store to purchase these materials before you begin making your fiber art jewelry:

VARIOUS FIBERS: thread, yarn, embroidery floss, hemp

VARIOUS EMBELLISHMENTS: beads, buttons, charms, shrink plastic pieces

JEWELRY ADHESIVE

BEADING NEEDLE: extremely small needle designed for stringing or sewing beads with small holes

NEEDLE THREADER: device used to thread needles with very small holes

BEADING THREAD

CRAFT SCISSORS

FIBER ART MATERIALS
(clockwise from top) colored yarn, various beads and charms, craft scissors

 ## WHAT TYPES OF FIBERS SHOULD BE USED?

Just about anything in your craft room is fair game, but different threads and fibers have diverse properties. Assemble your materials before putting them together to assess whether a bead looks best with heavily textured yarn, smooth metallic thread or another material.

Metallic threads come in a variety of colors and thicknesses. They are extremely durable, and thinner varieties pass easily through most bead holes. Their strength and flexibility make them ideal for lanyard knotting, knitting, braiding, macramé and crocheting.

Hemp is available in a limited color range, but has an earthy, natural appearance that complements ethnic-style jewelry. It's durable and easy to manipulate.

Yarn is available in a wide variety of colors, textures, weights and strengths. Thick yarn may be too bulky to pass through bead holes, while thin yarn may be too fragile to support heavy beads or charms. Heavily textured yarn is ideal for many jewelry projects, but not all. Embroidery floss can also be used, especially for the lighter-weight jewelry pieces favored by young girls. Combine several threads to make the piece stronger.

CARING FOR FIBER ART JEWELRY

Over time, fiber art jewelry may become soiled or pick up odors as it is worn against the skin. In most cases, however, it can be hand-washed with a gentle detergent and air-dried.

Test some fiber strands first to see how they react. High-quality fibers should stand up to the test well, but inexpensive yarn may "bleed" in the wash. As an alternative, spray it with a time-release fabric spray to control odors.

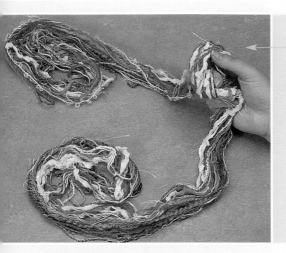

Braiding Techniques

A necklace or bracelet made of decorative fibers and charms will beautify any wardrobe. Surprisingly easy to make, you need only a few tools and materials to make a colorful fiber art jewelry set of your own.

Visit your local craft store, and you'll be amazed at the wide variety of colors, textures and styles they have to offer. Choose your fibers first, and then select beads to match. Or, bring your favorite charms, beads or buttons with you and find a fiber that will complement them.

1 PREPARE YOUR FIBERS
Select several strands of color-coordinated yarns and fibers and fold them in half as shown. Tie a large overhand knot in the center

2 TIE ADDITIONAL KNOTS
On each side of the loose middle knot, tie additional overhand knots. Pull tight.

3 BRAID THE FIBERS
Divide the fiber strands into three equal portions as shown, and braid them together.

4 FINISH THE BRAID
Continue braiding the strands until the necklace has reached the desired length. At the end of the braid, tie another overhand knot to keep it from coming undone. Repeat on the opposite side of the necklace.

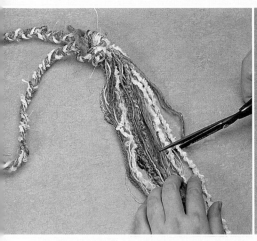

5 TRIM THE NECKLACE

Bring the two braided strands together, and tie or sew them in place. Then, tie a loose knot at the bottom, allowing the fibers to hang down like a tassel. Place the necklace flat on a work-table, and comb the loose fibers out with your fingers before trimming them evenly.

6 DESIGN THE NECKLACE

Place the necklace on a felt-covered jewelry design board. This makes it easy to place large buttons, beads and other embellishments on or near the necklace as you create your design.

7 SECURE THE EMBELLISHMENTS

Secure the embellishments by sewing them in place.

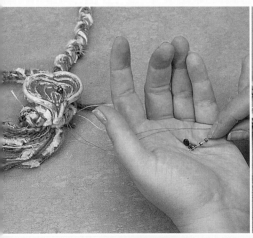

KNITTING AND CROCHETING TECHNIQUES

To knit or crochet a strand for a jewelry piece, use large knitting needles or a thick crochet hook and heavy fibers. After finishing each end, sew a medium-size button to one end with strong thread. Create a loop large enough for the button to pass through on the opposite end, sewing it down with beading thread to form a jewelry clasp.

8 ADD BEADS TO THE NECKLACE

Tie a knot in the end of doubled beading thread before you begin to sew beads onto the necklace. Run the needle through the necklace fibers and tie the threads in place with one or more knots. When the thread is secure, add a few beads.

9 SEW THE BEADS IN PLACE

Run the beaded thread around the fiber strands, and push the needle through the fibers to the other side. The beads on the thread should not pass through the fibers. Tie a knot on the other side of the fibers. Add more beads, and sew them in place on the fiber art necklace.

Knotting Techniques

Macramé, lanyard knots and other decorative knots also work in jewelry-making, but they require a lot of yarn or thread. Experiment with different techniques and keep your knotting simple to avoid making bulky jewelry.

1 BEGIN WITH A KNOT

Group color-coordinated fibers in strands of equal length. Tie a loose overhand knot near one end. Divide the strands into three groups as shown.

2 START THE MACRAMÉ CHAIN

Bring the left-hand group of strands crosswise over the middle strands of fiber as shown.

3 COMPLETE A KNOT

Bring the right-hand group of fiber strands over the crosswise strands from the previous step, and then under the middle group of strands.

4 PULL IT TOGETHER

Pull the strands to tighten the knot, but don't tie it too tight. A loose, flat knot is best for attaching beads and rubber stamped embellishments later.

5 TIE THE SECOND KNOT

Repeat the previous three steps, but start by bringing the right-hand fiber strands crosswise over the middle strands of fiber. Pull tight.

6 FINISH THE NECKLACE

Continue tying knots until you have the desired length, and then tie it off with a large overhand knot. Sew or glue on embellishments of your choice.

SHRINK PLASTIC

EMBELLISHMENTS

Shrink plastic is a versatile craft material that has been used for years by artists of all ages. Lately, it has come to the attention of rubber stamp artists who use it to make small charms, beads and embellishments. Shrink plastic may be colored before or after baking, and it is known for holding color extremely well. Shrink plastic may be stamped before and/or after shrinking it, and also painted afterward to create different effects.

 ## BASIC MATERIALS FOR SHRINK PLASTIC

A quick trip to the craft store is all you'll need to begin creating your own shrink art charms and embellishments:

SHRINK PLASTIC: manufactured plastic material that shrinks when heated; available in white, black, clear and translucent

320- TO 400-GRIT SANDPAPER: used to prepare shrink plastic for application of various pigments by roughing up the surface first

PIGMENT INK: see Basic Stamping Materials (page 30)

TEXTILE PAINTS: see Basic Stamping Materials (page 30)

NON-ACRYLIC SEALANT: seals the surface so colored pigments won't rub off

RUBBER STAMPS, INCLUDING HAND-CARVED RUBBER ERASERS

CRAFT SCISSORS

DECORATIVE-EDGED SCISSORS

HOLE PUNCH

CRAFT KNIFE

DEDICATED TOASTER OVEN: used to heat and shrink shrink plastic

EMBOSSING TOOL: see Basic Stamping Materials (page 30)

BAKING SHEET

JEWELRY ADHESIVE

OTHER INCLUSIONS: non-oil pastels, chalk, colored pencils, metallic rub-ons

SHRINK PLASTIC MATERIALS
(clockwise from top right)
embossing (heat) tool,
hole punch, colored
pencils, shrink plastic
in various colors

 ## WHAT IS SHRINK PLASTIC?

Shrink plastic is a manufactured plastic material that is first heated and stretched, and then sold in 8½" x 11" (21.6cm x 27.9cm) sheets. When heat is applied (in a toaster oven or with an embossing tool), the plastic shrinks approximately 45% and to a thickness of ⅟₁₆" (0.2mm).

Shrinking the plastic intensifies color applied while creating a lasting bond between the color and the plastic. Details are sharpened, colors are much more vibrant and saturated, and the miniaturizing effect makes finished pieces ideal for jewelry projects. Shrink plastic is available in white, black, clear and translucent.

WHY USE SHRINK PLASTIC?

Many artists and crafters enjoy using shrink plastic because it's an effective way to create small charms and embellishments with detailed designs and incredible color saturation. Almost any rubber stamp in your collection can be used to make small jewelry pieces. Shrink plastic is easy to use and requires no special tools or materials.

PREPARE THE SHRINK PLASTIC
Sand both sides of the plastic, and brush off the powdered residue before applying any color.

Preparing Shrink Plastic

To prepare shrink plastic for use, it is very important to sand it on both sides with 320- to 400-grit sandpaper or a sanding block. This helps the plastic "grab" color media such as chalks, pastels, watercolors, inks and paints.

Some shrink plastic is sold in a pre-sanded condition. But sanding is easy if you use a sanding block, which can be found in most hardware stores.

There is one exception to the sanding rule: clear shrink plastic should never be sanded. The scratches from the sandpaper will ruin the effect.

Baking Shrink Plastic

Bake shrink plastic on a baking sheet in a dedicated toaster oven at 300°F to 350°F (149°C to 177°C) for three to five minutes, or use an embossing tool to watch your pieces as they shrink to the desired size. Some artists find that the extremely high temperatures of the embossing tool cause their pieces to heat too rapidly. If you wish to try this method, move the tool around as you heat the plastic, keeping it 4" to 5" (10.2cm to 12.7 cm) away from the piece. Flip the plastic over to heat both sides evenly.

Sometimes shrink plastic will stick to itself during the heating process. This is because the plastic moves as it shrinks. Allow sticky plastic to cool before pulling it apart. Reheat to finish the shrinking process.

Decorating Shrink Plastic

When embellishing shrink plastic, most artists prefer using heat-set and pigment inks, textile paints, non-oil pastels and chalks, colored pencils, watercolors and metallic rub-ons. Dye-based ink is not recommended, and acrylic paint tends to puff up during shrinking.

1 APPLY COLOR TO THE PLASTIC
On sanded shrink plastic, stamp an image with black ink, applying chalks to the image with a makeup applicator sponge.

2 CUT OUT AND SHRINK THE IMAGE
Cut out the image with sharp scissors, punching a hole if needed, and shrink the plastic with an embossing tool or in a dedicated toaster oven.

STAMPING, CUTTING AND PUNCHING

Once a background color has been applied to the plastic, it is ready to stamp. Use pigment ink, heat-setting ink or textile paint to stamp in a random pattern or a deliberate design. Add more color to the stamped images as desired. Always keep the shrinkage factor in mind as you cut out each piece.

Use plain or decorative-edged scissors, a large paper punch or a sharp craft knife to cut out your shapes. For intricate cuts, use small scissors. For pieces with interior cuts (such as picture frames), use a sharp craft knife or paper punch to remove some of the plastic material.

NOTE

Shrink plastic is almost impossible to cut once it has been heated and shrunk, so trim off any sharp edges or points before applying heat.

If you intend to use your shrink plastic pieces as charms, use a standard paper hole punch to punch a hole in the plastic (about ⅛" to ¼" [0.3cm to 0.6cm] from the edge) prior to shrinking it.

1 APPLY THE BACKGROUND COLOR
Use a light application of color on both sides of the plastic.

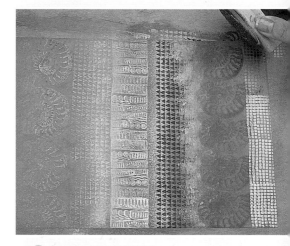

2 STAMP THE PLASTIC
Stamp repeat patterns horizontally or vertically in the colors and patterns of your choice.

3 CREATE THE CHARMS
Cut the plastic into various shapes. Trim off the sharp edges and punch holes in the charms.

4 SHRINK THE PLASTIC
Shrink each charm separately using an embossing tool (shown here) or a dedicated toaster oven.

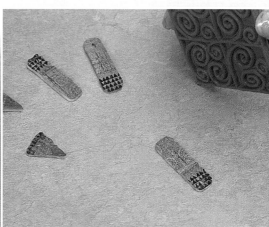

5 FLATTEN THE PLASTIC
Immediately flatten the surface of the plastic with a rubber stamp (shown here), a piece of matboard or a steel bench block.

SEALING SHRINK PLASTIC

Although heat melds color media to the surface of shrink plastic, you may want to seal the surface to be absolutely sure the colors will not rub off or run. Non-acrylic sealants (matte or glossy) are generally regarded as the best choice. Spray on a few light coats, allowing the surface to dry between coats.

You can also coat the finished piece in clear embossing ink and then dip it into clear, thick embossing powder as shown here. This will ensure that your shrink art jewelry pieces remain bright and beautiful for years to come.

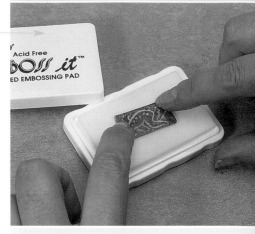

1 APPLY EMBOSSING INK
Apply the shrink plastic piece to a fresh pad of clear embossing ink. Add a heavy application of ink to both sides.

2 DIP IT IN POWDER
Use pliers or tweezers to dip the inked plastic into clear embossing powder.

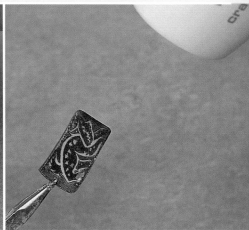

3 HEAT THE SHRINK PLASTIC
Heat the piece to melt the embossing powder, and immediately immerse it into the clear powder again. Heat again, immerse in more powder, and heat for a third and final time. Allow the piece to dry on a non-stick surface.

USING ADHESIVES

My best advice on adhering jewelry findings, beads or found objects to shrink plastic is to use a fine-quality product such as E6000. This is an industrial strength multi-purpose adhesive that bonds to porous and non-porous surfaces. Quick Stik adhesive pads and dots are also available, but they aren't as effective for adhering beads or stones. Ultra Thin Bond, a heat-activated dry adhesive, also works well.

CREATING INTAGLIO

A popular technique with rubber stamp artists is sometimes called intaglio, meaning "a design produced in relief." Start by coloring, stamping and shrinking your plastic pieces as usual. But instead of using a piece of matboard or steel bench block to flatten them, press them firmly with a rubber stamp or textured object for a few seconds. When you remove the stamp, it will leave a molded, textured impression in the surface of the plastic.

The look of intaglio-molded shrink plastic can be enhanced by daubing the raised areas with metallic rub-ons or by drybrushing the surface with metallic paints. Intaglio stamping does have a way of distorting the original stamped designs, however, so practice with this technique before attempting a final project.

MORE CREATIVE
EMBELLISHMENTS

Jewelry artists who use rubber stamps and related materials to make and embellish their creations find that the world is their art-supply store. While jewelry suppliers, bead stores and art-and-craft shops are very helpful resources, many materials for jewelry-making can be found in some rather unexpected places: stained-glass supply stores, yarn shops, and even hardware stores and home-improvement centers. In this section, we will focus on just a few of the many items that can be incorporated into your unique jewelry pieces.

BASIC MATERIALS FOR FOAM

CRAFT FOAM: product offered in a variety of shapes and colors; available in most craft stores

RUBBER STAMPS: including hand-carved rubber erasers

ACRYLIC PAINTS: see Basic Stamping Materials (page 30)

EMBOSSING TOOL: see Basic Stamping Materials (page 30)

BASIC MATERIALS FOR GLASS

GLASS: cut to size of jewelry piece; ask to have sharp edges ground smooth

COPPER TAPE: used to bind the edges of glass; available at stained-glass retail stores

CRAFT SCISSORS

OTHER INCLUSIONS: metallic paints, colored pencils, chalks and pastels

BASIC MATERIALS FOR COPPER

COPPER SHEET: available in jewelry supply stores

PERMANENT BLACK INKPAD

CRAFT SCISSORS

TWEEZERS

PETROLEUM JELLY

LIVER OF SULFUR: compound that, when mixed with hot water, darkens metal such as copper or silver

EMBOSSING STYLUS: sharp tool used for punching a stamped image into copper and other surfaces

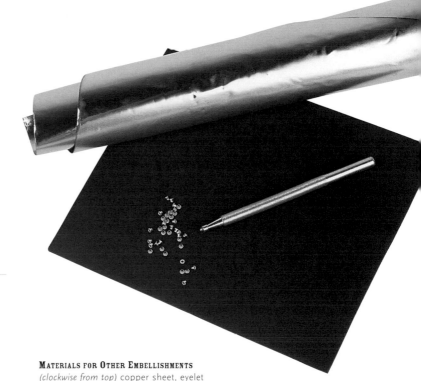

BASIC MATERIALS FOR EYELETS

EYELETS: small metal rings used to strengthen holes in materials such as paper, cardstock and shrink plastic

HOLE PUNCH

EYELET HAMMER: tool designed for hammering eyelets

MATERIALS FOR OTHER EMBELLISHMENTS
(clockwise from top) copper sheet, eyelet hammer, eyelets, foam

STAMPING ON CRAFT FOAM

Usually found in the children's department of craft stores or in large toy stores, craft foam is very useful to rubber stamp artists and jewelry designers alike.

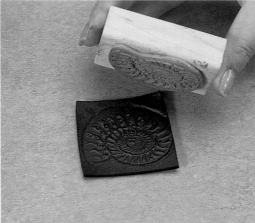

1 HEAT THE FOAM

Heat the surface of the foam with an embossing tool. Rotate the tool continuously to avoid scorching the foam.

2 STAMP ONTO CRAFT FOAM

Immediately press a rubber stamp (or alternative textured item) onto the surface and hold it there for a few seconds.

3 FINISH THE PIECE

Remove the stamp, cut out the image if desired, and apply metallic paints with a paintbrush or sponge.

STAMPING ON COPPER

Creating beautiful stamped images on copper is easier than you may think.

1 COAT THE STAMP

Coat a rubber stamp with petroleum jelly.

2 STAMP THE COPPER SHEET

Carefully impress a piece of copper sheet with the jelly-coated stamp, keeping in mind that the jelly makes the stamp a bit slippery.

3 DIP THE COPPER

Gripping the copper sheet firmly with a pair of tweezers or pliers, dip it into a solution of heated Liver of Sulfur.

4 RINSE THE COPPER

Remove the copper sheet once the Liver of Sulfur has blackened the surface. Rinse it in cool water and allow it to air-dry on a paper towel. Once the copper sheet has dried, wipe off the petroleum jelly and use the copper for jewelry projects.

EMBOSSING ON COPPER

All it takes to emboss a beautiful pattern onto a copper sheet is a rubber stamp, permanent ink, copper sheet and an embossing stylus. Try it for yourself to enhance any jewelry piece.

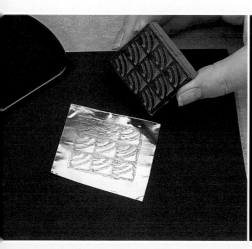

1 STAMP THE COPPER

Ink a stamp with black permanent ink and stamp it onto the copper sheet.

2 EMBOSS THE IMAGE

Use an embossing stylus to press the stamped pattern into the copper sheet. Work on a hard surface with a piece of craft foam beneath the copper sheet for cushioning.

3 FINISH THE PIECE

The finished embossed copper sheet may be trimmed and used for jewelry projects.

STAMPING ON GLASS

Small glass pieces are extremely useful for jewelry-making. They can be found in stained-glass supply stores, craft shops or online. Beveled-edge and faceted glass pieces are especially decorative.

  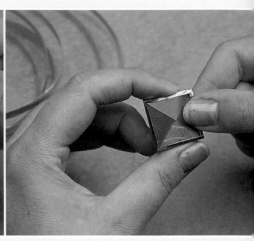

1 STAMP THE GLASS
Apply metallic paint to the surface of a rubber stamp. Place the stamp image-side up on a work surface, and carefully press the glass to the stamp. If the image blurs, quickly wipe off the paint and start over.

2 APPLY PAINT
Apply a contrasting color of paint to the back of the glass piece and allow it to dry.

3 APPLY COPPER TAPE
Use copper tape to create a frame around your stamped glass piece.

LAYERING WITH GLASS

You can also layer pieces of glass over stamped and decorated images. Frame them with copper tape for a miniature framed piece of art.

 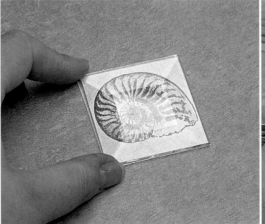 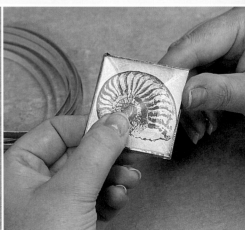

1 COLOR A STAMPED IMAGE
Use colored pencils, pastels or chalks to color a stamped image.

2 FIT THE GLASS
Center a piece of clear beveled glass over the stamped and colored image, trace around it lightly with a pencil, and cut out the image slightly within the lines.

3 ADHERE THE IMAGE
Use copper tape to adhere the stamped paper to the beveled glass. Trim the tape, rub the glass edges with a fingertip, and press the tape down along the top and bottom edges of the glass.

Using Eyelets

Eyelets are small metal rings available in various colors, sizes and shapes. Typically used in card making and scrapbooking, jewelry artists also find many uses for them, such as linking tiny sales tags together as shown here.

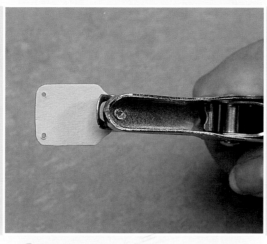

1 PUNCH HOLES
Start by punching small holes in the corners of tiny sales tags.

2 INSERT THE EYELETS
Lay the eyelets on a firm work surface. Place the tag over an eyelet and insert it through the hole.

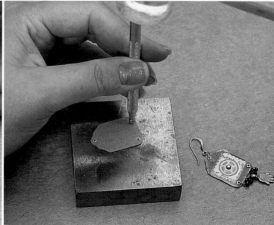

3 HAMMER THE EYELETS
On a steel bench block or other firm work surface, hammer the eyelets in place as shown. Use very light taps of the hammer to avoid smashing them.

left to right: I Love Paris {PAGE 84} · Wild Woman Dancing on a String {PAGE 56} · Heart and Hand {PAGE 108} · Down the Tubes {PAGE 90}
opposite page: Domino Adornments {PAGE 120} · Copper Sunrise {PAGE 94}

Now that you have been introduced to the nuts and bolts of jewelry construction, it's time for the fun part: the projects! Many talented stamp artists who enjoy crafting masterpieces in miniature contributed to this section, sharing their creative ideas and talents in jewelry-making so that others might benefit.

- A wide variety of media were used with rubber stamps and related materials to craft these unique pieces. In addition to the ever-popular polymer clay and shrink plastic, you will find that stamp artists are using natural fibers, acetate, vinyl tubing, copper sheet, wire, beveled glass pieces, eyelets, dominoes, craft foam and even tiny shipping tags to make beautiful pendants, necklaces, bracelets and earrings.

- Whether you're new to rubber stamping or a seasoned expert, you can expect to learn much by experimenting with the wide variety of media and techniques represented in this section. As one idea cross-pollinates with another, new jewelry forms will emerge and fresh ideas will be invented.

- You are invited to play with these new materials and techniques, asking yourself, "Hmm, what if I tried ...?" until you reach a number of satisfying conclusions. And if you should make a mistake? Rejoice—for that is when learning and personal growth truly begin.

- Several artists and crafters, each with their own individual style, contributed generously to this book. I hope you enjoy exploring their ideas and making them your own, adding your own personal touch to jewelry projects that will satisfy you for years to come.

WILD WOMAN DANCING ON A STRING
SHE'S ALIVE! THIS DANCING PENDANT MOVES WITH YOU.

A small art doll of stamped polymer clay is easily converted into a pendant with dangly appendages. The clay arms and legs appear to dance as the pendant is jiggled up and down, making this wearable art piece a conversation starter at any party. The artist made the doll's body by stamping randomly in a sheet of polymer clay, then cutting out a basic body shape before attaching appendages with beaded string.

GETTING STARTED

• *For detailed information on the processes used in making this piece, consult the sections on Getting Started with Jewelry-Making (page 8), Rubber Stamp Embellishments (page 30) and Polymer Clay Embellishments (page 33).*

pendant

- beads
- art stamps
- face button
- polymer clay: copper
- gold wire eye pins
- small clasp
- beading thread
- skewer
- craft knife
- metallic paint
- acrylic paint: black
- acrylic sealer: clear
- jewelry adhesive
- cornstarch
- toaster oven
- hand-cranked pasta machine or rolling pin

PROJECT BY: Debbie Shipley, Bowie, Maryland
STAMP COMPANY: Rubber Poet

PENDANT

1 Condition clay as described in Polymer Clay Embellishments, page 34. Roll it out into a large ¼" (0.6cm) thick slab, and then stamp into it with various images. Cut out a rectangular shape with a rounded end for the head.

2 Use a skewer to punch holes in the clay for the dangling arms and legs.

3 Form two hands and two legs from polymer clay, and insert gold wire eye pins into each end.

4 Make a mold for a polymer clay face: form a ball of scrap clay, and push a face button into the ball. Remove the button, and bake the clay mold. To create the polymer clay face, dust the inside of the mold with cornstarch, and push raw clay into the mold. Remove the face carefully.

5 Place the face, body, arms and hands in a 275°F (135°C) oven, and bake for 25 minutes. Remove and allow to cool. Pull out the eye pins, apply jewelry adhesive to the ends, and reinsert them into the arms and legs.

6 Use scrap clay from steps 1 to 3 to form rollup beads on the skewer. See Polymer Clay Embellishments, page 39, for instructions. Remove the skewer and bake at 275° (135°C) for 25 minutes.

7 Antique the beads with black acrylic paint (the artist recommends using Lumiere), and add highlights with metallic paint. Seal the pieces with clear acrylic sealer. For antiquing instructions, see Polymer Clay Embellishments (page 37).

8 When all the pieces are painted and dried, connect the legs and feet to the body with beading thread strung with beads. String more beads onto the thread and attach the hands, small beads and clay rollup beads from step 6. Attach the units to the body, and glue the clay face to the top of the body.

9 String beading thread with various beads as desired.

10 Attach a small clasp.

PROJECT BY: Leslie Altman, Deerfield, Illinois
STAMP COMPANIES: Embossing Arts, Inkadinkado, Marks of Distinction, Postmodern Design,
Rubber Stampede, Stampers Anonymous, Toybox Rubber Stamps

VENUS & DECORES

AN OLD CRAFT FAVORITE—FRIENDLY PLASTIC—
IS PAIRED WITH FOAM AND STAMPS.

Friendly Plastic was once a very popular craft medium, but after a time it seemed to go out of style. It can be difficult to find in your local craft store (see the Resources section on page 124 for product information), but thanks to the popularity of rubber art stamps, Friendly Plastic is back in high demand with jewelry designers. The metallic finish and pliability of the heated plastic make it ideal for creating beautiful, enduring artistic brooches and pendants like those pictured above.

GETTING STARTED

• *For detailed information on the processes used in making these pieces, consult the section on Rubber Stamp Embellishments (page 30).*

• *Use parchment paper for a non-stick surface when working with Friendly Plastic.*

PENDANTS & BROOCHES

pendants & brooches

- Friendly Plastic: 7″ (17.8cm) strips each of metallic solid copper/black and metallic solid orange copper/black
- art stamps
- found objects
- craft foam: black
- parchment paper
- pin-backs
- gold or silver chain
- decorative-edged scissors
- metallic paint
- gel pens, various colors
- gold leafing pen
- powdered pigments
- dimensional lacquer
- cotton-tipped applicator
- hairspray
- acrylic nail polish: clear
- embossing fluid: clear
- jewelry adhesive
- spray adhesive
- embossing tool

1 Cut out a piece of craft foam to the shape of the rubber stamped image you will be using. A rectangular shape is probably easiest to work with for the first time.

2 Use an embossing tool to heat each side of the foam, for a total of three passes. Immediately press the art stamp into the foam and hold it down for a few seconds with even pressure.

3 Cut out another piece of foam the same size and shape as the first one, and glue the two together with jewelry adhesive.

4 Trim the assembled piece as necessary with decorative-edged scissors.

5 Lightly sponge on metallic paint (the artist recommends using Lumiere) in bronze or the color of your choice. Use a cotton-tipped applicator to apply tiny amounts of powdered pigments (the artist recommends using Pearl Ex) to the surface to enhance the design. Apply a few light coats of hairspray to fix the powders in place.

6 Add highlights with an aqua gel pen, or the color of your choice, and a gold leafing pen.

7 The base structure of the jewelry is copper Friendly Plastic. Working on parchment paper, cut several strips of plastic the same size as the foam, and several pieces slightly larger than the foam. Make sure you have enough for a double thickness. This will provide a thick layer in which to embed the embossed foam from steps 1 to 6.

8 Place two pieces of plastic side by side, and melt them together by applying heat to the surface with an embossing tool. Don't overheat the plastic. It should have a crackled finish when ready. Layer more pieces of plastic onto the melted pieces and reheat.

9 Quickly press the embossed foam piece from steps 1 to 6 into the thick, melted plastic. While it is still warm, mold and form the melted plastic so that it covers the sides of the foam and creates a base. Flattened areas of melted plastic may be impressed with rubber stamps or found objects to create texture. Always coat such objects with clear embossing fluid to create a release agent, or the plastic may stick to them.

10 Allow the piece to cool, and decorate the surface with a gel pen or gold leafing pen.

11 Apply a coat of clear acrylic nail polish to the surface to seal it. Add a few layers of dimensional lacquer (the artist recommends using 3-D Crystal Lacquer) to create a thick, shiny surface.

TIPS

- *Small charms, beads and found objects may be adhered to the front of the piece after it has cooled and dried. Try drilling small holes near the bottom of the piece and using jump rings to attach bead dangles and charms.*

- *To keep the melted plastic from sticking to your fingers, rub on a little clear embossing fluid before handling it.*

TAG ART

TINY SALES TAGS MAKE THIS JEWELRY SET PRICELESS.

Miniature collages of rubber stamped imagery on sales tags might seem a bit unusual to some of us, but for paper artists, it's the natural thing to do. These tiny tags are just the right size for adorning your neck, wrist and earlobe. Laminating the paper before assembling the jewelry is the trick. Incorporate little beads, rhinestones, turquoise chips and chains, and you've got a memorable piece of paper jewelry.

GETTING STARTED

• *For detailed information on the processes used in making these pieces, consult the sections on Getting Started with Jewelry-Making (page 8) and Rubber Stamp Embellishments (page 30).*

PROJECT BY: Tami Rodrig, Lexington, Massachusetts
STAMP COMPANIES: Hero Arts, Lasting Impressions, Nina Bagley Designs, Renaissance Art Stamps, Stampa Rosa, Stampers Anonymous, Stampington and Company, Zettiology

necklace

- sales tags measuring ³⁄₄″ x 1¹⁄₄″ (1.9cm x 3.2cm)
- gold or silver cardstock
- paper
- art stamps
- beads or turquoise chips
- wire
- clasp
- chain
- chain-nose pliers
- round-nose pliers
- hole punch
- craft scissors
- dye inkpads
- gold or silver leafing pen
- crayons, colored pencils or pens
- jewelry adhesive

NECKLACE

1 Stamp various images onto paper and cut them out in different shapes.

2 Glue the tiny paper shapes to seven small sales tags measuring ³⁄₄″ x 1¹⁄₄″ (1.9cm x 3.2cm).

3 Add spots of color by cutting out or punching tiny scraps of decorative paper and gluing them on as well.

4 Use crayons, colored pencils or pens to add color as needed.

5 Glue the sales tags to gold or silver cardstock, allow them to dry, and then cut them out. Run a gold or silver leafing pen around the edge of each tag.

6 Laminate the tags and cut them out.

7 Use a small hole punch to punch tiny holes in the top of each tag.

8 Create jump rings for each tag as described in Getting Started with Jewelry-Making (page 12). Attach the tags to the chain and add various beads. Attach a clasp.

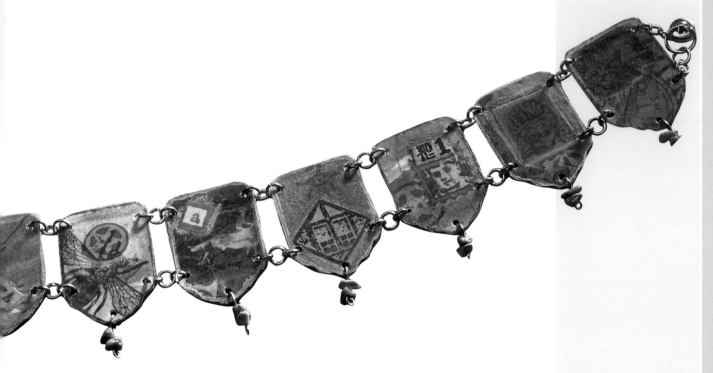

Bracelet

1 Stamp various images onto paper and cut them out in different shapes.

2 Glue the paper shapes to seven sales tags measuring ³⁄₄″ x 1¹⁄₄″ (1.9cm x 3.2cm).

3 Add spots of color by cutting out or punching tiny scraps of decorative paper and gluing them as well.

4 Use crayons, colored pencils or pens to add color as needed.

5 Glue the sales tags to gold or silver cardstock, allow them to dry, and then cut them out. Run a gold or silver leafing pen around the edge of each tag.

6 Laminate the tags and cut them out.

7 Use a small hole punch to punch tiny holes in the top and on both sides of each tag.

8 Create jump rings for each tag as described in Getting Started with Jewelry-Making (page 12), and attach the tags to each other. Dangle tiny beads or turquoise chips from each tag by making a wire bead dangle.

9 Attach a clasp.

b r a c e l e t

- sales tags measuring ³⁄₄″ x 1¹⁄₄″ (1.9cm x 3.2cm)
- gold or silver cardstock
- paper
- art stamps
- beads or turquoise chips
- wire
- clasp
- chain-nose pliers
- round-nose pliers
- hole punch
- craft scissors
- dye inkpads
- gold or silver leafing pen
- crayons, colored pencils or pens
- jewelry adhesive

EARRINGS

1 Stamp various images onto paper and cut them out in different shapes.

2 Glue the tiny paper shapes to two small sales tags measuring ³⁄₄″ x 1¹⁄₄″ (1.9cm x 3.2cm).

3 Add spots of color by cutting out or punching tiny scraps of decorative paper and gluing them on as well.

4 Use crayons, colored pencils or pens to add color as needed.

5 Glue the sales tags to gold or silver cardstock, allow them to dry, and then cut them out. Run a gold or silver leafing pen around the edge of each tag.

6 Laminate the tags and cut them out.

OPTION: glue a rhinestone to the surface of each tag.

7 Use a small hole punch to make tiny holes at the top and bottom of each tag.

8 Create jump rings for each tag as described in Getting Started with Jewelry-Making (page 12), and attach the tags to earring hooks. Dangle beads or turquoise chips from the base of each earring by stringing them on a wire and running the ends through the two holes at the bottom of each tag.

earrings

- sales tags measuring ³⁄₄″ x 1¹⁄₄″ (1.9cm x 3.2cm)
- gold or silver cardstock
- paper
- art stamps
- beads, turquoise chips and rhinestones
- wire
- earring hooks
- chain-nose pliers
- round-nose pliers
- hole punch
- craft scissors
- dye inkpads
- gold or silver leafing pen
- crayons, colored pencils or pens
- jewelry adhesive

TIP

Laminating the tags makes them stronger and able to withstand more wear and tear. Small laminating machines are often sold in rubber stamp and scrapbook stores, but you can also laminate large sheets of paper at your local photocopy store.

PUTTIN' ON THE RITZ

SHRINK ART AND POLYMER CLAY—IT'S A MATCH MADE IN HEAVEN.

Stamped shrink plastic marries well with black polymer clay adorned with variegated gold leaf. Wrapped with beaded copper wire and attached to gorgeous specialty yarns and fibers, this necklace, brooch and earring set is a showstopper. The long necklace looks particularly beautiful against a plain black dress, and the earrings are dainty enough to coordinate with any outfit. The brooch dresses up a tailored lapel.

GETTING STARTED

•*For detailed information on the processes used in making these pieces, consult the sections on Getting Started with Jewelry-Making (page 8), Rubber Stamp Embellishments (page 30) Fiber Art Embellishments (page 41) and Shrink Plastic Embellishments (page 45) .*

•*This project is completed in two parts: making the shrink art charms and embellishments and incorporating them into a necklace, earrings and brooch jewelry set.*

charms & embellishments

•shrink plastic: black
•polymer clay: black
•art stamps: art deco designs
•needle tool
•⅛" (0.3cm) hole punch
•400-grit sandpaper
•craft scissors
•craft knife
•crafter's ink
•acrylic paint
•metallic inks
•variegated gold leaf
•jewelry adhesive
•clear acrylic spray
•toaster oven
•hand-cranked pasta machine or rolling pin

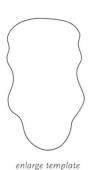

enlarge template 200%

CHARMS ℔ EMBELLISHMENTS

1 Prepare black shrink plastic by sanding it with 400-grit sandpaper. Cut out several pieces in pleasing shapes (one for the brooch, three for the necklace), or use the template provided below. You will need to enlarge the template for the brooch and necklace on a photocopier, but keep in mind that there will be approximately 45% shrinkage when baked.

2 Stamp the shrink plastic in the center of each cutout plastic piece using a large art deco image and Crafter's ink. Mask off the image with paper. Stamp smaller images around the central image, and remove the paper mask. Punch two holes near the bottom of the largest shrink plastic piece.

3 Heat the plastic pieces in a toaster oven at 275°F (135°C) for a few minutes, removing the pieces when they're completely shrunk.

4 Use additional stamps for more images if desired. When finished, seal each piece with acrylic spray. Set aside.

5 Condition and roll out two large slabs of black polymer clay on the #1 setting of a hand-cranked pasta machine, or roll it out by hand to ⅛" (0.3cm) thickness.

6 Cover one slab of raw clay with gold leaf, and gently pressing it into place with your fingertips. Cut several long strips about ¼" (0.6cm) wide and set them aside.

7 Place the prepared shrink art pieces on the black polymer clay, and use a craft knife to cut around each shape, adding a ¼" (0.6cm) border around each piece. Remove excess clay.

8 Press the strips from step 6 around the perimeter of the shrink art pieces to frame them. Press the seams together to seal. Use additional strips of gold leafed clay to form arches on each charm.

9 Remove the shrink art pieces from the polymer clay frames, and bake the frames. When the frames have cooled, affix the shrink art pieces to them with jewelry adhesive.

10 To make small charms, embellishments and dangles for earrings, simply stamp images randomly over prepared black shrink plastic, cut them out, punch holes as needed, and shrink.

(CON'T ON NEXT PAGE)

PROJECT BY: Louise Duhamel, Carlsbad, California
STAMP COMPANIES: Hero Arts, Judi-Kins

11 To create polymer clay disk beads, roll out black clay to about ⅛″ (0.3cm) thick. Sponge acrylic paint onto assorted rubber stamps, and stamp the images into the clay, pressing firmly but not deeply. Wait 10 minutes for the paint to dry, and then cut out small round shapes. Use a needle tool to punch two holes near the center of each disk. Make larger beads with thicker clay.

12 Use leftover scraps of clay to form tubular beads. Cut the scraps into manageable pieces, and wrap them around a needle tool to form tube shapes.

13 Bake the disk beads and tube beads for 20 to 25 minutes at 275°F (135°C), remove from the oven and allow to cool.

BROOCH

1 Run copper wire through the hole in the bottom of the large charm and the top of the small shrink art dangle charm (see steps 1 to 9 in Charms & Embellishments, page 65). Attach the two together.

2 Use extra-long round-nose pliers to coil and design a decorative dangle.

3 String assorted small beads and crystals onto copper wire, and coil the ends to secure the beads. Make two or three strands in this manner. See Getting Started with Jewelry-Making (page 15) for coiling instructions.

OPTION: Beads may be strung on beading thread instead of copper wire.

4 Assemble a collection of decorative fibers with the beaded strands, and run them through the arch at the top of a large charm. Tie a knot to secure.

5 Adhere a pin-back with jewelry adhesive. Allow to dry for 24 hours before wearing.

brooch

- beads and crystals
- fibers and threads
- one large charm
- one shrink art dangle charm
- pin-back
- 20-gauge copper wire
- extra-long round-nose pliers
- jewelry adhesive
- toaster oven
- hand-crank pasta machine or rolling pin

EARRINGS

1 Create two shrink art dangle charms as described in Charms & Embellishments (page 65). Punching a ⅛″ (0.3cm) hole at the top of each charm before shrinking.

2 Make small jump rings from 20-gauge copper wire with your round-nose pliers. See Getting Started with Jewelry-Making (page 12) for help.

3 String three to five small beads and crystals onto a short piece of 20-gauge copper wire. Coil the ends to secure them.

4 Run the jump rings through the holes in the shrink art dangles and attach the beaded wire. Finally, open the eye pin at the bottom of each earring wire and attach one to each beaded shrink art dangle.

earrings

- assorted beads and crystals
- small charm dangles
- earring wires
- 20-gauge copper wire
- chain-nose pliers
- round-nose pliers
- toaster oven

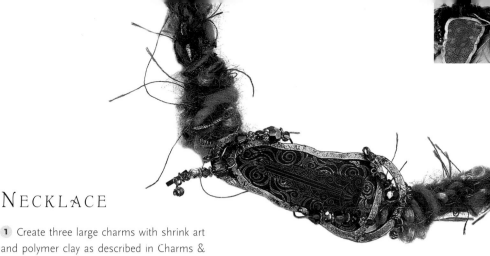

Necklace

1 Create three large charms with shrink art and polymer clay as described in Charms & Embellishments (pages 65 to 66), punching ⅛″ (0.3cm) holes near the top of each piece. Bake in a toaster oven to shrink. Set aside.

2 Choose various fibers, and cut each to approximately 3' to 4' (0.9mm to 1.2mm). Attach the fibers to the centerpiece charm from step 1 by tying them with a slipknot through the top arch. Allow a 5″ (12.7cm) tail of fibers to dangle to the side. Tie a knot of fibers beneath the charm, and add strung beads and crystals as desired.

3 Divide the necklace fibers into two groups to form each necklace strand. Using lanyard or macramé knots and braids, fashion a long necklace.

4 About 5½″ (14cm) from the central large charm, attach two more large charms with slip knots. Continue braiding and knotting as before until the necklace is of the desired length.

5 Run the fibers behind the large charm, and secure them at the bottom by coiling the ends of 20-gauge copper wire. Attach a small shrink art charm if desired. Continue braiding and knotting.

6 Use copper wire to attach small shrink art charms, polymer clay disk beads, and other assorted beads and crystals. To attach disk beads, fold a piece of wire in half, place the fibers in the "V" of the fold, and run the wire ends through the holes in the bead. These beads may also be attached with beading thread and a needle.

7 Wrap additional wire with beads and crystals around the large charms as shown, coiling the ends to secure the beads.

8 Add long strands of coiled wire with beads and shrink art charms randomly by wrapping the wire around the knotted and braided fibers.

9 Tie off the loose ends with tight knots, and trim off excess fibers. Make two eye pins as described in Getting Started with Jewelry-Making (page 18), with 16-gauge wire, and run one through each knot.

10 Dot the top of each knot with glue, and add a tubular bead. On the opposite end of each tubular bead, form another eye pin with the back of your extra-long round-nose pliers, and attach a toggle clasp.

TIPS

- *You may use an embossing tool instead of a toaster oven to shrink plastic. If necessary, flatten the hot plastic with a piece of cardboard.*

- *This jewelry set requires some planning ahead. First, select the fibers in coordinating colors. Choose colors that complement each other and the wire you will be using. Then, choose stamping ink and acrylic paint colors that coordinate with the chosen fibers. Metallics are especially nice.*

- *Silver or colored wire may be substituted for copper wire.*

ORIENTAL ORNAMENTS

THIS JEWELRY SET HAS A DECIDEDLY ORIENTAL ORIENTATION.

For this project, the artist used a single stamp image with a harlequin diamond pattern. This type of pattern stamp is easy to use in numerous ways, illustrating that artists are never limited to using their rubber stamps as is! Combined with unusual items like decorative toothpicks, this jewelry set is both simple and sophisticated. The artist created an Asian look by using rich, red, earth-toned chalks.

GETTING STARTED

• For detailed information on the processes used in making these pieces, consult the sections on Getting Started with Jewelry-Making (page 8), Rubber Stamp Embellishments (page 30) and Shrink Plastic Embellishments (page 45).

NECKLACE

necklace

- shrink plastic: clear
- art stamp
- assorted beads
- bead stringing thread
- clasp
- 26-gauge gold wire
- chain-nose pliers
- round-nose pliers
- craft scissors
- hole punch
- toothpicks
- earth-toned chalks
- permanent ink: black
- jewelry adhesive
- embossing tool or toaster oven

1 Stamp an image four times on the clear shrink plastic with black permanent ink. Cut out and color the backs of the plastic with earth-toned chalks.

2 Shrink two of the pieces as they are, using an embossing tool or toaster oven. With the third piece, cut off the three end squares so that the piece is smaller than the first two, and then shrink it. With the fourth piece, cut three squares in a V-shape. Cut out two small, individual squares, and punch holes near the top corner of each. Shrink all the pieces. Allow them to cool, pressing flat with cardboard if necessary. Set aside.

3 Glue 18 decorative toothpicks side by side as shown and allow to dry. Wrap gold wire around the two outer toothpicks, and add a drop of glue if necessary. Spiral the ends away from the toothpicks to dangle jump rings.

4 String assorted beads to create a necklace, adding a clasp. Attach the ends of the necklace to the wire wrapped around the toothpicks.

5 String assorted beads onto two pieces of 1½″ (3.8cm) of 26-gauge gold wire, and make eye pins on each end. Make four jump rings with gold wire. For instructions on making jump rings, see Getting Started with Jewelry-Making (page 12).

6 Follow the guidelines in Getting Started with Jewelry-Making (page 24) for attaching the dangles to the necklace with jump rings. Attach the beaded dangle to two jump rings, and attach those jump rings to the coiled wire on the toothpicks.

7 Assemble the shrink plastic pieces on the toothpicks as shown, using jewelry adhesive to hold them in place. Glue down the two largest pieces first, overlapping slightly, and then the next smallest pieces just beneath them. Finish with the small V-shaped plastic piece. Once glued, allow the necklace to dry for 24 hours before wearing.

PROJECT BY: Heather Crossley, Stretton Heights, Queensland, Australia
STAMP COMPANY: Stampers Anonymous

This project illustrates just how versatile a single stamp can be. Go through your own stamp collection, and choose a few images that you haven't used for a while. Stamp each a few times with black ink on paper, and then cut out the images. Cut these images into smaller pieces, and rearrange them on your worktable in pleasing combinations. See how creative you can be with just a few images cut in unusual ways. Then, try making an art piece by stamping on shrink plastic, cutting the pieces in abstract shapes, and affixing the shrunken pieces in various combinations.

Earrings

1 Stamp an image five times on the clear shrink plastic with black permanent ink. Cut out and color the backs of the plastic with earth-toned chalks.

2 Cut out seven squares from four of the five pieces you cut out in step 1. Place the squares, two by two, back to back. Orient the pieces vertically, and punch holes near the top and bottom of each set. From the fifth image, cut out four small squares from the design. Punch a hole near the top corner of each to make tiny dangles.

3 Shrink the plastic pieces with an embossing tool or in a toaster oven. Allow them to cool, pressing flat with cardboard if necessary. Use jewelry adhesive to glue the larger pieces back to back, taking care to line up the holes. Set them aside.

4 String assorted beads onto two 1" (2.5cm) pieces of 26-gauge gold wire, and make eye pins on each end. Make four jump rings with gold wire. For instructions on making jump rings, refer to Getting Started with Jewelry-Making (page 12).

5 Follow the guidelines in Getting Started with Jewelry-Making (page 24) for attaching the tiny dangles from step 2 to the eye pins and shrink art pieces, which are then attached with jump rings to the earring wires.

earrings
- shrink plastic: clear
- art stamp
- assorted beads
- earring wires
- 26-gauge gold wire
- chain-nose pliers
- round-nose pliers
- craft scissors
- hole punch
- earth-toned chalks
- permanent ink: black
- jewelry adhesive
- embossing tool or toaster oven

BROOCH

brooch

- shrink plastic: clear
- art stamp
- assorted beads
- pin-back
- 26-gauge gold wire
- chain-nose pliers
- round-nose pliers
- craft scissors
- hole punch
- jewelry adhesive
- earth-toned chalk
- permanent ink: black
- embossing tool

1 Stamp an image twice on the clear shrink plastic with black permanent ink. Cut out and color the backs of the plastic with earth-toned chalks.

2 On the first piece, punch four holes near the bottom of the plastic for dangles. On the second piece, cut out four squares from the design, and punch a hole near the top corner of each.

3 Shrink the plastic pieces with an embossing tool or in a toaster oven. Allow them to cool, pressing flat with cardboard if necessary.

4 String assorted beads onto four 2" (5.1cm) pieces of 26-gauge gold wire. Make eye pins on each end. Make eight jump rings with gold wire. For instructions on making jump rings, see Getting Started with Jewelry-Making (page 12).

5 Follow the guidelines in Getting Started with Jewelry-Making (page 24) for attaching the dangles to the brooch with jump rings.

6 Adhere a pin-back on the back of the brooch and allow to dry for 24 hours before wearing.

AN EYE FOR AN EAR...OR A NECK

OPTOMETRIST LENSES MAKE GREAT PENDANTS.

What's the latest rage in mixed-media artifacts for assemblage jewelry? Vintage optometrist lenses! First used during the early 1900s to prescribe eyeglasses, the lenses are encased in different metals such as nickel and brass, with glass that may be clear, partially frosted or colored. The metal tabs may be simple or very ornate, and they are often punched at the top with tiny holes. This makes it easy to suspend them on earring wires, jump rings, thin leather strands or various fibers. Many stamping, embossing and coloring techniques may be used, and even the simplest approaches will render stunning results.

GETTING STARTED

For detailed information on the processes used in making these pieces, consult the chapters on Getting Started with Jewelry-Making (page 8), Rubber Stamp Embellishments (page 30) and Fiber Art Embellishments (page 41).

earrings
- optometrist lenses
- art stamps
- paper
- earring wires
- chain-nose pliers
- craft scissors
- clear-drying glue
- pencil
- inks and chalks

necklace
- optometrist lenses
- art stamps
- paper
- fibers
- beads and charms
- chain-nose pliers
- round-nose pliers
- craft scissors
- clear-drying glue
- pencil
- inks and chalks
- jewelry adhesive

EARRINGS

1 Stamp and color ordinary craft paper.

2 Place the lenses on various parts of the paper, allowing the frame on the lens to guide your placement. When you find a pleasing composition within the frame, trace around it very lightly with a pencil and cut out the circle.

3 Glue two stamped circles back to back and allow to dry.

4 Use glue around the edge of each lens to adhere the paper circle to it.

5 Glue two prepared lenses back to back, allowing the stamped picture to show through on each side.

6 Use chain-nose pliers to open the eye pin on the bottom of an earring wire and run it through the hole in the top of the metal lens tab. Close the eye pin.

NECKLACE

1 Stamp and color ordinary craft paper.

2 Place the lenses on various parts of the paper, allowing the frame on the lens to guide your placement. When you find a pleasing composition within the frame, trace around it very lightly with a pencil and cut out the circle.

3 Glue two stamped circles back to back and allow to dry.

4 Use glue around the edge of each lens to adhere the paper circle to it.

5 Glue two prepared lenses back to back, allowing the stamped picture to show through on each side. Run fibers or jump rings through the hole in the top of each metal lens tab. See Getting Started with Jewelry-Making (page 12) for help.

6 Braid, crochet or macramé a necklace of fibers, and attach the lenses to it with strands of fiber. Finish the necklace by adding glass beads and charms.

PROJECT BY: Carolyn Waitt, Huntington Beach, California
STAMP COMPANIES: Acey Deucy, Ornamentum, Stampington & Company, Zettiology

PROJECT BY: Julie Pearson, Traverse City, Michigan
STAMP COMPANY: All stamps designed by the artist from public-domain sources and hand-drawn imagery.

RENAISSANCE IMPRESSIONS

A BEAUTIFUL ANTIQUE FINISH LENDS A RENAISSANCE FLAIR TO THESE TINY COMPOSITIONS.

T iny, intricate artworks easily translate into wearable art for the lapel. Because they're so small, it's easy to overlook the details. Note that some of these brooches feature tiny color photocopies of ancient paintings, while others are decorated with brass charms and rhinestones. In every case, careful placement of the elements is the key to success.

GETTING STARTED

• *For detailed information on the processes used in making these projects, consult the chapters on Rubber Stamp Embellishments (page 30) and Polymer Clay Embellishments (page 33).*

• *Use a color photocopier to reduce artwork, photographs, found art, etc. Trim to size; the finished artwork should measure no larger than 1″ (2.5cm) square.*

BROOCHES

1 Condition polymer clay as directed in Polymer Clay Embellishments (page 34). Roll out conditioned clay to about ⅛″ (0.3cm) thickness.

2 Using a black archival inkpad (the artist recommends using Memories archival ink), stamp various images onto black or white clay. If desired, brush the top of the clay with metallic watercolor pigments.

3 Use a sharp craft knife to cut the clay into small squares, rectangles and other shapes. Reassemble them to create small compositions. Layer the clay pieces if desired. Small triangles and strips of stamped clay may also be placed on top of larger pieces to create 3-dimensional compositions.

4 In the center of each brooch, cut out an opening measuring ½″ (1.3cm) square. The opening may be slightly larger to accommodate larger pieces of art, but must not be bigger than your largest glass squares.

5 Bake the clay brooches at 275˚F (135˚C) for about 25 minutes. Remove them from the oven and allow to cool.

6 Place a baked brooch on a piece of heavy watercolor paper, and trace around it. Remove the brooch, and cut out the piece of watercolor paper, which will become the backing for the brooch.

NOTE: The paper backing must be at least as large as the clay brooch, but it may also extend beyond the boundaries of the clay.

7 Paint both sides of the paper cutout with black gesso and allow to dry completely. This not only colors the paper, but also stiffens it and provides a protective coating to make a nice backing for the brooch.

8 Place the clay piece on the watercolor backing piece. Then, place a photocopied and reduced image within the cutout square opening from step 4, and affix the clay and photocopied artwork to the backing piece with clear-drying glue. Allow the glue to dry.

9 Clean a small glass piece, removing dust and fingerprints. Place it on the clay brooch, covering the photocopied artwork. When satisfied with the placement, adhere the glass with glue (the artist recommends using Elmer's Stix-All). If excess glue oozes out, remove it with a toothpick, or apply metallic pigments to the glue for an interesting effect.

10 Adhere small brass charms, beads, rhinestones, tiny wire coils, watch parts, glass mosaic pieces, micro-beads and other found objects to the surface of the brooch. Because the finished brooch is small, keep these elements to a minimum.

11 Affix a pin-back to the back of the brooch and allow to dry for 24 hours before wearing.

TIPS

• Postage stamps may be substituted for color-photocopied artwork.

• Placing a glass square over the miniature artwork is optional but recommended to protect the paper art from the elements.

• To dangle small beads and charms, drill a tiny hole at the bottom of the clay brooch after it has been affixed to the paper backing. Use wire and pliers to create jump rings and bead dangles as described in Getting Started in Jewelry-Making (page 12).

• The finished brooches may be converted into necklace pendants by affixing a bail to the back instead of a pin-back.

MODERN MEMORIES

PHOTO STAMPS ARE USED TO MIMIC VINTAGE JEWELRY.

Once you master the technique of stamping on copper, you'll find a multitude of uses for it in your jewelry projects. By stamping with a thin coating of petroleum jelly, you create a barrier on the copper that protects it from oxidizing. Immersing the stamped copper sheet into a solution of Liver of Sulfur, you'll be amazed at how quickly it turns a lovely "antiqued" black on the surface. When the petroleum jelly barrier is wiped away, it reveals a beautifully stamped image in shimmering copper.

GETTING STARTED

•*For detailed information on the processes used in making these pieces, consult the section on Copper Sheet Stamping (page 50).*

PROJECT BY: Renee Plains, Scottsdale, Arizona
STAMP COMPANIES: Stampers Anonymous, Stampotique Originals

pendant

- chipboard
- rubber stamp: script design
- ⅛" (0.3cm) thick basswood
- paper: cream
- clear plastic(styrene) sheet
- prepared copper sheet
- ¼" (0.6cm) silver foil tape
- fine cord: black
- clear plastic ruler
- bone folder
- eye pin
- jump ring
- pin vise
- round-nose pliers
- chain-nose pliers
- craft scissors
- ⅝" (1.6cm) hole punch
- ink: black
- chalk: tan
- archival inkpad: brown
- clear-drying glue

PENDANT

1 Follow the instructions in Copper Sheet Stamping (page 50) to prepare a copper sheet. Cut a 1" (2.5cm) square from the prepared copper sheet.

2 Stamp a photo art stamp with brown archival ink (the artist recommends using Memories ArtPrint Brown archival ink) on cream-colored paper. Once dry, rub on a little tan chalk. Cut out a 1" (2.5cm) square, using a clear plastic ruler so you can center an image in the square.

3 Stamp a script stamp with black ink on chipboard, and cut out a 1" (2.5cm) square. Center and punch a ⅝" (1.6cm) hole.

4 Cut out one 1" (2.5cm) square each of the clear plastic sheet and the basswood.

5 Layer the central charm in this order: copper from step 1 (stamp side down), basswood from step 4, photo stamp image from step 2, clear plastic from step 4, and chipboard from step 3. Glue the layers together along the edges. Once dry, add silver foil tape and burnish all edges with a bone folder.

6 Add a charm or bead dangle to the bottom of the pendant by drilling a tiny hole into the bottom of the square with a pin vise and inserting an eye pin with glue. For help with this, see Getting Started with Jewelry-Making (page 18).

7 Drill a second hole in the top of the square, insert another eye pin and add a jump ring. See Getting Started with Jewelry-Making (page 12) for help. String the pendant on a fine black cord or a silver chain.

EARRINGS

1 Follow the instructions in Copper Sheet Stamping (page 50) to prepare a copper sheet. Cut two ³⁄₄″ (1.9cm) squares from the prepared copper sheet.

2 Stamp a photo art stamp with brown archival ink (the artist recommends using Memories ArtPrint Brown archival ink) on cream-colored paper. Once dry, rub on a little tan chalk. Cut out two ³⁄₄″ (1.9cm) squares, using a clear plastic ruler so that you can center an image in each square.

3 Stamp a script stamp with black ink on chipboard, and cut out two ³⁄₄″ (1.9cm) squares. Center and punch a ¹⁄₂″ (1.3cm) hole inside each square.

4 Cut out two ³⁄₄″ (1.9cm) squares each of the clear plastic sheet and the basswood.

5 Layer the earring charms in this order: copper from step 1 (stamp side down), basswood from step 4, photo stamp image from step 2, clear plastic from step 4, and chipboard from step 3. Glue the layers together along the edges. Once dry, add silver foil tape and burnish all edges with a bone folder.

6 Use a pin vise to drill tiny holes at the tops of each charm, and insert the eye pin. For eye pin instructions, refer to Getting Started with Jewelry-Making (page 18). Add glue if needed to secure the eye pins in the charms. Dangle from earring hooks.

earrings

- chipboard
- rubber stamps:
  script design, photo art
- ¹⁄₈″ (0.3cm) thick basswood
- paper: cream
- clear plastic (styrene) sheet
- prepared copper sheet
- ¹⁄₄″ (0.6cm) silver foil tape
- clear plastic ruler
- bone folder
- earring hooks
- eye pins
- pin vise
- craft scissors
- ¹⁄₂″ (1.3cm) hole punch
- ink: black
- chalk: tan
- archival inkpad: brown
- clear-drying glue

TIP

Liver of Sulfur is an organic compound used by jewelry artists to "antique" certain metals such as copper and silver. It can be purchased from bead retailers and through jewelry supply catalogs. See the Resources section for information.

bracelet

- chipboard
- snaps: black
- art stamps:
  script design, photo art
- ¼" (0.6cm) silver foil tape
- ⅛" (0.3cm) thick basswood
- paper: cream
- 28-gauge tin sheet metal
- clear plastic (styrene) sheet
- prepared copper sheet
- clear plastic ruler
- bone folder
- craft scissors
- ⅝" (1.6cm) hole punch
- ink: black
- chalk: tan
- archival inkpad: brown
- clear-drying glue

Bracelet

1 Follow the instructions in Copper Sheet Stamping (page 50) to prepare a copper sheet. Cut a strip measuring 6½" x ¾" (16.5cm x 1.9cm) and a 1" (2.5cm) square out of the prepared copper sheet. Cut a strip of 28-gauge tin sheet metal measuring 6½" x ¾" (16.5cm x 1.9cm).

2 Glue the tin and copper strips together, and immediately wipe off any residue. Allow the strips to adhere and dry completely before proceeding.

3 Use ¼" (0.6cm) silver foil tape to wrap the edges of the strip, centering the foil tape and folding over all the edges. Burnish the tape with a bone folder.

4 Curve the strip into the form of a bracelet that fits your wrist. Set aside.

5 Stamp a photo art stamp with brown archival ink (the artist recommends using Memories ArtPrint Brown archival ink) on cream-colored paper. Once dry, rub on a little tan chalk. Cut out a 1" (2.5cm) square, using a clear plastic ruler so that you can center an image in the square.

6 Stamp the script stamp with black ink on chipboard, and cut out a 1" (2.5cm) square. Center and punch a ⅝" (1.6cm) hole in the chipboard.

7 Cut one 1" (2.5cm) square each out of the clear plastic sheet and the basswood.

8 Layer the central charm in this order: copper from step 1 (stamp side down), basswood from step 7, photo stamp image from step 5, clear plastic from step 7 and chipboard from step 6. Glue the layers together along the edges. Once dry, add silver foil tape and burnish all edges with a bone folder.

9 Glue the charm to the center of the bracelet, and add six black snaps (or other embellishments of your choice) as shown.

MEDIEVAL ITALIAN GEMS

SOLDERING AND STAMPING TINY GLASS BEVELS IS AN EASY WAY TO MAKE MEDIEVAL JEWELRY.

They sparkle like precious gems, but on closer inspection prove to be rubber stamped jewels made of beveled glass and permanent inks. By soldering the edges and applying a patina solution to them, you can fashion jewelry that appears to be hundreds of years old and is fit for a queen.

GETTING STARTED

•*For detailed information on the processes used in making these pieces, consult the sections on Getting Started with Jewelry-Making (page 8) and Rubber Stamp Embellishments (page 30).*

•*You can find small glass bevels for this project in many craft stores and through stained-glass suppliers.*

•*The process for making the beveled glass pieces in this project is the same. To save time, you may want to make several at once prior to assembling the individual jewelry pieces.*

PROJECT BY: Carol Heppner, Marlton, New Jersey
STAMP COMPANIES: Acey Deucy, Stampers Anonymous, The Stamping Ground, The Stampsmith

necklace
- beads
- charms
- art stamps
- one glass bevel 1" (2.5cm) square
- two glass bevels ½" (1.3cm) square
- beading wire
- two head pins
- clasp
- 26-gauge gold wire
- copper tape
- flux
- toothpaste
- toothbrush
- foam brush
- cotton balls
- chain-nose pliers
- round-nose pliers
- copper and black patina (optional)
- soldering iron
- lead-free solder
- permanent inks: gold, blue and green
- spray sealer

NECKLACE

1 Secure copper tape around all four edges of each glass bevel. Place the bevels on a non-flammable work surface.

2 Apply flux to the copper tape. Run a bead of solder around the copper-taped edge, turn the glass bevel over, and apply flux to the tape on that side as well.

3 Solder around the taped edge, making sure that all sides of the glass bevel are coated with solder.

4 Solder a jump ring to one-corner of each bevel as shown. For instructions on creating jump rings, refer to Getting Started with Jewelry-Making (page 12).

5 Once the pieces have cooled, use a toothbrush and toothpaste to clean the flux from the surface of the glass bevel. Dry the pieces with a soft cloth.

OPTION: Apply copper patina to the soldered edges with a cotton ball, and dry with a soft cloth. Black patina may then be applied to the copper patina.

6 Stamp the back of the glass bevel with gold ink (the artist recommends using Décor-it ink) and allow to dry.

7 Apply blue and/or green ink to the entire back of the glass bevel with a foam brush and allow to dry. Apply a spray sealer.

8 String small beads and charms on beading wire or thread. Make a bead dangle as described in Getting Started with Jewelry-Making (page 24), and attach this to the 1" (2.5cm) square bevel, then to a brass charm.

9 Attach the brass charm to the necklace with jump rings. The two small bevel charms may be attached to the necklace with jump rings about 1½" (3.8cm) from the brass charm dangle.

10 Attach a clasp.

Earrings

1 Secure copper tape around all four edges of each glass bevel. Place the bevels on a non-flammable work surface.

2 Apply flux to the copper tape. Run a bead of solder around the copper-taped edge, turn the glass bevel over, and apply flux to the tape on that side as well.

3 Solder around the copper-taped edge, making sure that all sides of the glass bevel are coated with solder.

4 Solder a jump ring to opposite corners of each bevel as shown. For instructions, see Getting Started with Jewelry-Making (page 12).

5 Once the pieces have cooled, use a toothbrush and toothpaste to clean the flux from the surface of the glass bevel. Dry the pieces with a soft cloth.

OPTION: Apply copper patina to the soldered edges with a cotton ball, and dry with a soft cloth. Black patina may then be applied to the copper patina.

6 Stamp the back of the glass bevel with gold ink (the artist recommends using Décor-it ink) and allow to dry.

7 Apply blue and/or green ink to the entire back of the glass bevel with a foam brush and allow to dry. Apply a spray sealer.

8 Make two small bead dangles as described in Getting Started with Jewelry-Making (page 24).

9 Attach the glass dangles to earring hooks with head pins. For instructions, see Getting Started with Jewelry-Making (page 23).

earrings

- beads
- art stamps
- two glass bevels ½" (1.3cm) square
- earring hooks
- jump rings
- 26-gauge gold wire
- flux
- toothpaste
- toothbrush
- foam brush
- copper tape
- cotton balls
- copper and black patina (optional)
- soldering iron
- chain-nose pliers
- round-nose pliers
- lead-free solder
- permanent inks: gold, blue and green
- spray sealer

TIP

Copper tape, soldering irons, solder and flux can be purchased at a stained-glass store. Beginners will have more success if they learn how to solder in a stained-glass class before attempting this project. Such workshops are offered through community colleges and the parks and recreation departments in many cities.

bracelet

- beads
- charms
- art stamps
- four glass bevels ½"
  (1.3cm) square
- clasp
- 26-gauge gold or silver wire
- flux
- toothpaste
- toothbrush
- foam brush
- copper tape
- cotton balls
- copper or black patina
  (optional)
- soldering iron
- lead-free solder
- chain-nose pliers
- round-nose pliers
- permanent inks: gold,
  blue and green
- spray sealer

BRACELET

1 Secure copper tape around all four edges of each glass bevel. Place the bevels on a non-flammable work surface.

2 Apply flux to the copper tape. Run a bead of solder around the copper-taped edge, turn the glass bevel over, and apply flux to the tape on that side as well.

3 Solder around the copper-taped edge, making sure that all sides of the glass bevel are coated with solder.

4 Solder a jump ring to opposite corners of each bevel as shown. For instructions, see Getting Started with Jewelry-Making (page 12).

5 Once the pieces have cooled, use a toothbrush and toothpaste to clean the flux from the surface of the glass bevel. Dry the pieces with a soft cloth.

OPTION: Apply copper patina to the soldered edges with a cotton ball, and dry with a soft cloth. Black patina may then be applied to the copper patina.

6 Stamp the back of the glass bevel with gold ink (the artist recommends using Décor-it ink) and allow to dry.

7 Apply blue and/or green ink to the entire back of the glass bevel with a foam brush and allow to dry. Apply a spray sealer.

8 Assemble the glass bevels together with jump rings, adding bead dangles and small jewelry charms as desired. For instructions, refer to Getting Started with Jewelry-Making (page 12).

9 Attach a clasp.

I LOVE PARIS

FRAME YOUR MINIATURE STAMP ART BEHIND GLASS.

The creator of this jewelry set enjoys making soldered glass jewelry pieces because they are so versatile and the design choices are practically limitless. With literally thousands of rubber stamp images to choose from, your next jewelry project will be as unique as your imagination. Your stamping technique may be as simple or as elaborate as you choose, and framing your design behind glass will turn it into a work of wearable art.

GETTING STARTED

- *For detailed information on the processes used in making these pieces, consult the section on Rubber Stamp Embellishments (page 30).*
- *Have a glass shop cut the required glass, grinding the edges so that the copper tape will adhere.*
- *Prepare your work surface by covering it with clean newspaper.*

bracelet

- 7/8" x 5/8" (2.2cm x 1.6cm) pre-cut glass, 1/16" (0.2cm) thick, 10 pieces
- beads, silver charms (optional)
- cardstock
- art stamps
- cotton balls
- bone folder
- rubbing alcohol
- brush
- clasp
- copper tape
- flux
- soldering iron
- chain-nose pliers
- round-nose pliers
- rosin core solder 60/40
- chalks, colored pencils and pens
- ink

BRACELET

1 Using your favorite stamping techniques, create tiny works of art on cardstock and color them with chalks, colored pencils or pens. Reduce them on a color photocopier if necessary. To check for the correct size, lay a piece of 7/8" x 5/8" (2.2cm x 1.6cm) pre-cut glass on top of your artwork. Trim off any excess paper. Repeat 10 times to create five glass charms for a medium-sized bracelet.

2 Cut copper tape to size. Use glass cleaner to clean the glass pieces, sandwich your artwork between two pieces of glass, and wrap the edges with copper tape. Use a bone folder to burnish the sides and corners of the tape to the glass. Repeat four times to create a total of five glass charms.

3 Apply flux to the copper tape sparingly with a small brush. Using a soldering iron and solder, melt the solder around the perimeter of the glass and sides.

4 When the pieces cool, turn them over and solder the backs. Using chain-nose pliers to hold jump rings, solder one ring to both short sides of each glass piece. For instructions on how to create a jump ring, refer to Getting Started with Jewelry-Making (page 12). Thoroughly remove the flux from the glass using a cotton ball and rubbing alcohol.

5 Attach the glass charms to one another with additional jump rings. If using long, oval-shaped jump rings, you can attach small beads, crystals and silver charms as well. These will dangle nicely between the glass charms.

6 Finish the bracelet with the clasp of your choice.

PROJECT BY: Suzie Heinzel, Newnan, Georgia
STAMP COMPANY: Tin Can Mail

PENDANT

1 Using your favorite stamping techniques, create tiny works of art on cardstock and color them with chalks, colored pencils or pens. Reduce them on a color photocopier if necessary. To check for the correct size, lay a piece of 1½″ x 2″ (3.8cm x 5.1cm) pre-cut glass on top of your artwork. Trim off any excess.

2 Cut copper tape to size. Use glass cleaner to clean two pieces of glass, sandwich your artwork between them, and wrap the edges with copper tape. Use a bone folder to burnish the sides and corners of the tape to the glass.

3 Repeat steps 1 and 2 with two glass pieces 2″ (5.1cm) in diameter.

4 Apply flux to the copper tape sparingly with a small brush. Using a soldering iron and solder, melt the solder around the perimeter of the glass and sides.

5 When the pieces cool, turn them over and solder the backs. Using chain-nose pliers to hold jump rings, solder one ring to the top of each piece, and one more jump ring to the bottom of the rectangular piece. For instructions on how to make jump rings, refer to Getting Started with Jewelry-Making (page 12). Remove the flux from the glass using a cotton ball and rubbing alcohol.

6 Connect the two glass pieces with an additional jump ring. Tie a ribbon in place with a bead embellishment. Run a necklace chain through the jump ring at the top of the rectangular piece.

pendant

- 1½″ x 2″ (3.8cm x 5.1cm) pre-cut glass, 1/16″ (0.2cm) thick, 2 pieces
- 2″ (5.1cm) diameter circles pre-cut glass, 1/16″ (0.2cm) thick, 2 pieces
- beads
- cardstock
- art stamps
- brush
- cotton balls
- rubbing alcohol
- bone folder
- flux
- chain
- copper tape
- soldering iron
- chain-nose pliers
- round-nose pliers
- rosin core solder 60/40
- chalks, colored pencils and pens
- ink

BROOCH

brooch

- 1½″ x 2″ (3.8cm x 5.1cm) pre-cut glass, ¹⁄₁₆″ (0.2cm) thick, 2 pieces
- beads and ribbons
- cardstock
- art stamps
- brush
- cotton balls
- rubbing alcohol
- bone folder
- flux
- copper tape
- soldering iron
- pin-back
- chain-nose pliers
- round-nose pliers
- rosin core solder 60/40
- chalks, colored pencils and pens
- ink
- jewelry adhesive

1 Using your favorite stamping techniques, create tiny works of art on cardstock and color them with chalks, colored pencils or pens. Reduce them on a color photocopier if necessary. To check for the correct size, lay a piece of 1½″ x 2″ (3.8cm x 5.1cm) pre-cut glass on top of your artwork. Trim off any excess paper.

2 Cut copper tape to size. Use glass cleaner to clean two pieces of glass, sandwich your artwork between them, and wrap the edges with copper tape. Use a bone folder to burnish the sides and corners of the tape to the glass.

3 Apply flux to the copper tape sparingly with a small brush. Using a soldering iron and solder, melt the solder around the perimeter of the glass and sides. Using chain-nose pliers to hold a jump ring, solder the ring to the bottom of the glass piece.

4 When the piece cools, turn it over and solder the back. Remove the flux from the glass using a cotton ball and rubbing alcohol.

5 Embellish your piece using small beads, ribbon or whatever you desire by attaching them to the jump ring at the bottom of the glass piece.

6 Affix a pin-back to the back of the brooch with strong jewelry adhesive (the artist recommends using E6000). Allow the brooch to dry for 24 hours before wearing.

TIPS

- *Use small letter stamps to stamp sentiments and dates.*

- *For an antique effect on solder, brush on Novacan Black Patina (available in stained-glass stores).*

PROJECT BY: Linda Reid, North Providence, Rhode Island
STAMP COMPANY: The Stampsmith

FUN FOAM MAGIC

TURN A COMMON CRAFT MATERIAL INTO COOL JEWELRY.

Fun Foam is a type of craft foam that is easily found in stores craft and rubber stamping stores. When exposed briefly to high temperatures, Fun Foam becomes malleable and readily holds stamped impressions. For these pieces, the artist stamped into black double-thick Fun Foam, and then cut it into geometric shapes. Applying metallic rub-ons will highlight the surface design.

GETTING STARTED
• *For detailed information on the processes used in making these pieces, consult the sections on Getting Started with Jewelry-Making (page 8), Rubber Stamp Embellishments (page 30) and More Creative Embellishments (page 49).*

88   FUN FOAM MAGIC

bracelet

- Fun Foam: black, double-thick
- art stamps
- jewelry cord
- clasp
- jump ring
- fine-gauge gold wire
- hole punch or awl
- scissors or craft knife
- metallic rub-ons: copper and gold
- embossing tool

earrings

- Fun Foam: black, double-thick
- art stamps
- earring wires
- fine-gauge gold wire
- scissors or craft knife
- hole punch or awl
- metallic rub-ons: copper and gold
- embossing tool

pendant

- Fun Foam: black, double-thick
- art stamps
- jewelry cord
- decorative metal corners
- scissors or craft knife
- hole punch or awl
- metallic rub-ons: copper and gold
- jewelry adhesive
- embossing tool

brooch

- Fun Foam: black, double-thick
- art stamps
- pin-back
- scissors or craft knife
- metallic rub-ons: copper and gold
- jewelry adhesive
- embossing tool

BRACELET

1 Cut out a piece of Fun Foam measuring 2¾" x 1" (7cm x 2.5cm). Heat with an embossing tool, and quickly press an art stamp into the foam. Remove it after a few seconds.

2 Trim the piece closely around the stamped impression. Punch a hole through each end, approximately ¼" (0.6cm) from the edge.

3 Apply metallic rub-ons to the raised foam. Use sparingly.

4 Run 7" (17.8cm) of jewelry cord through each hole, and double back to create two strands on each end. Tie it off with a knot.

5 Attach a large jump ring and clasp to opposite ends of the jewelry cord with fine-gauge (22- to 24-gauge) wire. Wrap it tightly around the cord ends, and then around the jump ring and clasp.

EARRINGS

1 Cut out two pieces of Fun Foam measuring 1" [2.5cm] square each. Heat with an embossing tool, and quickly press an art stamp into the foam. Remove after a few seconds.

2 Punch a hole through one end of each charm, approximately ¼" (0.6cm) from the edge.

3 Attach a large jump ring and clasp to opposite ends of the jewelry cord with fine-gauge (22- to 24-gauge) wire. Wrap it tightly around the cord ends, and then around the jump ring and clasp.

4 Attach earring wires to each dangle with 22- to 24-gauge wire.

PENDANT

1 Cut out one piece of Fun Foam measuring 2" [5.1cm] square each. Heat with an embossing tool, and quickly press an art stamp into the foam. Remove after a few seconds.

2 Punch a large hole through one corner, about ¼" (0.6cm) from the edge.

3 Attach a large jump ring and clasp to opposite ends of the jewelry cord with fine-gauge (22- to 24-gauge) wire. Wrap it tightly around the cord ends, and then around the jump ring and clasp.

4 Use jewelry adhesive to affix decorative metal corners or charms of your choice to the front of the pendant.

5 Run about 30" (76.2cm) of jewelry cord through the hole, and tie a slipknot to attach the pendant to the cord. Tie off the ends.

BROOCH

1 Cut out one piece of Fun Foam measuring 2" [5.1cm] square. Heat with an embossing tool, and quickly press an art stamp into the foam. Remove it after a few seconds.

2 Trim the piece closely around the stamped impression. Punch a hole through each end, approximately ¼" (0.6cm) from the edge.

3 Apply metallic rub-ons to the raised foam. Use sparingly.

4 Affix a pin-back to the back of the brooch with jewelry adhesive. Allow to dry for 24 hours before wearing.

TIP

Substitute dry-brushed metallic acrylic paint for rub-ons. Dip a paintbrush in metallic paint, brush most of the color onto a paper towel, and apply to the surface of the impressed fun foam.

DOWN THE TUBES

VINYL TUBING IS THE SECRET BEHIND THIS FASHIONABLE JEWELRY SET.

Vinyl tubing may not be the first material one thinks of when contemplating a set of rubber stamped jewelry, but in the hands of artist Elizabeth Smithwa, this ordinary material becomes the stuff of contemporary magic. By inserting fibers or rolled, stamped papers into the tubing, and connecting it to beads and charms with wire, you can make long necklaces, short chokers, pretty bracelets, earring dangles and more.

GETTING STARTED

•For detailed information on the processes used in making these pieces, consult the sections on Getting Started with Jewelry-Making (page 8) and Rubber Stamp Embellishments (page 30).

necklace

- vinyl tubing, ¼″ (0.6cm), ⅜″ (1cm) and ½″ (1.3cm) in diameter
- beads and charms, including disk beads
- assorted yarns and fibers
- smooth paper (such as bond paper)
- art stamps
- small clasp
- 20-gauge wire
- flush cutters
- chain-nose pliers
- round-nose pliers
- craft scissors
- skewer
- sponge
- permanent inkpad: black
- inkpad: butterscotch
- embossing tool

PROJECT BY: Elizabeth Smithwa, Mission Viejo, California
STAMP COMPANIES: Uptown Rubber Stamps, All Night Media

NECKLACE

1 Sponge butterscotch-colored ink onto the paper to color it lightly and add an "antique" glaze to the surface. Allow it to dry, or heat-set with an embossing tool. Stamp images with black permanent ink to cover the entire sheet of paper, and heat-set again.

2 Cut out strips from the stamped paper, each about 1½″ (3.8cm) long and 1⅛″ (2.9cm) wide.

3 To prepare vinyl beads, cut ¼″ (0.6cm) diameter tubing about 9″ (22.9cm) long (for the tube that runs around the back of the neck) with scissors. Cut one piece of ½″ (1.3cm) diameter tubing about 1⅛″ (2.9cm) long. Cut two pieces of ⅜″ (1cm) diameter tubing, each 1⅛″ (2.9cm) long.

4 Roll a paper strip from step 2 on a skewer. Then, insert the skewer into a vinyl bead from step 3 that measures 1⅛″ (2.9cm), and release. The strip will uncurl until it meets the inside of the vinyl tubing. Repeat with the remaining two beads that measure 1⅛″ (2.9cm) long. Set aside.

5 For the tubing at the back of the neck, cut yarn and fibers about 11″ (28cm) long, and cut a 12″ (30.5cm) piece of 20-gauge wire with flush cutters. Using round-nose pliers, create a small loop at one end of the wire. String the fibers through the loop, and push the wire through the tubing like a needle, leading with the cut end.

6 When the tube is filled with yarn, release the yarn from the loop and straighten the wire. Re-thread the wire through the tubing, taking care not to push out the fibers. Stop pushing when 1½″ (3.8cm) of wire protrudes from each end of the tubing. Cut the fibers flush with the ends of the tubing. Add small beads to the protruding wires, and then form an eye pin loop at each end as described in Getting Started with Jewelry-Making (page 18). This will secure the beads in place.

7 Cut lengths of 20-gauge wire, and insert them into the three 1⅛″ (2.9cm) long vinyl beads. Add disk beads and additional small beads of your choice, and form an eye pin loop at each end to secure the beads in place.

8 To assemble, make jump rings as shown in Getting Started with Jewelry-Making (page 12). Connect the long neck tubing with beads or charms, then with the short tubing beads. Add more beads and charms as desired. Use the largest ½″ (1.3cm) diameter tubing for the central bead. Add dangling charms to the eye pin loops near the central bead. A simple clasp is located near the end of the neck tubing. Use pliers to attach the clasp.

EARRINGS

1 Sponge butterscotch-colored ink onto the paper to color it lightly and add an "antique" glaze to the surface. Allow it to dry, or heat-set with an embossing tool. Stamp images with black permanent ink to cover the entire sheet of paper, and heat-set again.

2 Cut out two strips from the stamped paper, each 1½" (1.3cm) long and ¾" (1.9cm) wide.

3 Cut ¼" (0.6cm) diameter vinyl tubing to make two beads, each ¾" (1.9cm) long.

4 Roll paper strips from step 2 on a skewer. Then, insert the skewer into the vinyl beads from step 3, and release. The strip will uncurl until it meets the inside of the vinyl tubing.

5 Place three small beads onto a 1½" (3.8cm) head pin, and insert them into one of the tubing beads. For instructions, refer to Getting Started with Jewelry-Making (page 23).

6 Add one more small bead, and close the loop at the top of the head pin. Repeat with the second tubing bead. Set the beads aside.

7 Create two small U-shaped dangles with 18-gauge wire, ending the U with closed loops as shown. Dangle a tubing bead from one loop and a bead or charm from the other, using jump rings as needed. For instructions, refer to Getting Started with Jewelry-Making (page 12). Repeat with the second U-shaped dangle.

8 Attach the U-shaped dangles to earring hooks.

earrings

- vinyl tubing, ¼" (0.6cm) in diameter
- beads and charms
- art stamps
- smooth paper (such as bond paper)
- earring hooks
- 18-gauge wire
- two 1½" (3.8cm) head pins
- flush cutters
- chain-nose pliers
- round-nose pliers
- craft scissors
- skewer
- sponge
- permanent inkpad: black
- inkpad: butterscotch
- embossing tool

TIPS

• *If you have trouble cutting the vinyl tubing with ordinary scissors, try metal shears or inexpensive kitchen shears.*

• *Remember to use good-quality wire cutters, and always flush cut each end of the wire when making eye pins and jump rings.*

BRACELET

1 Sponge butterscotch-colored ink onto the paper to color it lightly and add an "antique" glaze to the surface. Allow it to dry, or heat-set with an embossing tool. Stamp images with black permanent ink to cover the entire sheet of paper, and heat-set again.

2 Cut out four strips from the stamped paper, each 1½″ (3.8cm) long and ½″ (1.3cm) wide.

3 Cut ³/₈″ (1cm) diameter vinyl tubing to make four beads, each ½″ (1.3cm) long.

4 Roll paper strips from step 2 on a skewer. Then, insert the skewer into the vinyl beads from step 3, and release. The strip will uncurl until it meets the inside of the vinyl tubing.

5 Insert 20-gauge wire into each vinyl tubing bead, add a small silver bead at each end, and close each end of the wire with an eye pin. For instructions on how to create an eye pin, refer to Getting Started with Jewelry-Making (page 18).

6 On a piece of 20-gauge wire about 1½″ (3.8cm) long, string several disk-shaped beads, and secure them on the wire by closing each end with an eye pin.

7 Cut four pieces of 20-gauge wire, each about 1″ (2.5cm) long, and string three small silver beads or charms on the wire. Secure the beads by closing each end with an eye pin.

8 Assemble the bracelet by connecting the tubing beads with the beads made from steps 6 and 7. Add a clasp, and try the bracelet on for size. To enlarge the bracelet, add more tubing beads or small commercial beads. Remove beads as needed to make the bracelet smaller.

COPPER SUNRISE

HEAT BRINGS OUT THE RESPLENDENT BEAUTY OF COPPER FOIL AND METAL-EMBOSSING TECHNIQUES.

A favorite craft material of many jewelry artists is copper foil, or thin copper sheets that can be rubber stamped, embossed and torched with a flame to bring brilliant colors to the surface of the metal. Your design options are only limited by your rubber stamp collection! Once you try this technique, you'll find many more applications for it. The pendant pictured, for example, easily converts into a brooch.

GETTING STARTED

•*For detailed information on the processes used in making these pieces, consult the sections on Getting Started with Jewelry-Making (page 8) and Rubber Stamp Embellishments (page 30).*

PROJECT BY: Doris Arndt, Tacoma, Washington
STAMP COMPANIES: Rubber Stamp Plantation

necklace

- •beads
- •art stamp
- •one 2″ (5.1cm) square mirror
- •22-gauge copper wire
- •necklace cord
- •mouse pad
- •36-gauge copper foil
- •¼″ (0.6cm) copper foil tape
- •embossing stylus
- •flush cutters
- •chain-nose pliers
- •round-nose pliers
- •craft scissors
- •butane torch
- •inkpad: black
- •acrylic paint: black

NECKLACE

1 Cut two lengths of wire, 1½″ (3.8cm) each, with flush cutters. Bend each wire in half with the chain-nose pliers, and create a loop at the bend. Open the "legs" of the wire into a V-shape, and set aside.

2 Cut out a piece of copper foil 2½″ (6.4cm) square. Using the black inkpad, stamp a design on the back of the copper foil piece in the center of the square.

3 Place the copper square on a mouse pad, image side up, and go over the design with an embossing stylus. Press firmly, but not so hard that you penetrate the foil.

4 Heat the copper foil with a butane torch, which causes the metal to change color. Dip the copper in a bowl of water periodically to cool it, and then reheat as necessary to obtain the desired colors. Allow the copper foil to cool completely.

5 Apply black metallic rub-ons (the artist recommends using Rub-n-Buff) or acrylic paint over the embossed surface of the copper foil, polishing off the excess with a rag.

6 Turn the copper piece over (embossed side down) and place a 2″ (5.1cm) square mirror in the center. Miter the corners of the foil by trimming with scissors.

7 Place two wire lengths from step 1 between the copper foil and the mirror, allowing the loops to extend beyond the corners as shown. Fold each side of the copper foil over the edges of the mirror.

8 Apply copper foil tape to the edges of the folded copper piece, covering the raw copper edges. Buff the surface with a rag.

9 Cut three short but varying lengths of copper wire with flush cutters. String two beads on each, form a coil at one end to secure the beads, and form an eye pin loop on the opposite end of each wire. For instructions, refer to Getting Started with Jewelry-Making (page 18). Attach the eye pin loops to the loop extending from the bottom of the copper piece as shown.

10 String a long necklace cord through the loop extending from the top of the copper piece, and secure with a knot.

EARRINGS

1 Cut four lengths of wire, 1½" (3.8cm) each, with flush cutters. Bend each wire in half with the chain-nose pliers, and create a loop at the bend. Open the "legs" of the wire into a V-shape, and set aside.

2 Cut out two pieces of copper foil, each 1½" (3.8cm) square. Using the black inkpad, stamp a design on the back of each copper foil piece, in the center of the square.

3 Place one copper square on a mouse pad, image side up, and go over the design with an embossing stylus. Press firmly, but not so hard that you penetrate the foil. When finished, emboss the second sheet of foil.

4 Heat both copper pieces with a butane torch, which causes the metal to change color. Dip the copper in a bowl of water periodically to cool it, and then reheat as necessary to obtain the desired colors. Allow the copper to cool completely.

5 Apply black metallic rub-ons (the artist recommends using Rub-n-Buff) or acrylic paint over the embossed surface of the copper foil, polishing off the excess with a rag.

6 Turn the copper pieces over (embossed side down) and place a 1" (2.5cm) square mirror in the center of each. Miter the corners of the foil by trimming with scissors.

7 Place two wire lengths from step 1 between the copper foil and the mirror, and each copper piece, allowing the loops to extend beyond the corners as shown. Fold up each side of the copper foil over the edges of the mirrors.

8 Apply copper foil tape to the edges of the folded copper pieces, covering the raw copper edges. Buff the surface with a rag.

9 Cut two short lengths of copper wire, and insert two beads on each. Make loops at the end of each wire with pliers to make bead dangles. Attach a bead dangle to each copper piece as shown, and use chain-nose pliers to attach earring hooks.

earrings

- beads
- art stamp
- two 1" (2.5cm) square mirrors
- 36-gauge copper foil
- ¼" (0.6cm) copper foil tape
- mouse pad
- earring hooks
- 22-gauge copper wire
- embossing stylus
- flush cutters
- chain-nose pliers
- round-nose pliers
- craft scissors
- butane torch
- inkpad: black
- acrylic paint: black
- metallic rub-ons

TIPS

• It should be easy to cut 36-gauge copper foil with ordinary scissors, but don't use fine sewing shears for this project. Instead, use inexpensive kitchen shears, metal shears or old sewing scissors with dull blades.

• When heating copper foil, keep in mind that metal conducts heat. Grip the metal piece with rubber-handled pliers or a similar tool to avoid burning your fingers.

Bracelet

bracelet

- beads
- art stamp
- two 1" square mirrors
- one 1" (2.5cm) diameter round mirror
- 36-gauge copper foil
- 1/4" (0.6cm) copper foil tape
- mouse pad
- clasp
- 22-gauge copper wire
- flush cutters
- chain-nose pliers
- round-nose pliers
- craft scissors
- butane torch
- inkpad: black
- acrylic paint: black

1 Cut six lengths of wire, 1½" (3.8cm) each, with flush cutters. Bend each wire in half with the chain-nose pliers and create a loop at the bend. Open the "legs" of the wire into a V-shape, and set aside.

2 Cut out three pieces of copper foil, each 1½" (3.8cm) square. Stamp a design on the back of each copper foil piece, in the center of the square.

3 Place one copper square on a mouse pad, image side up, and go over the design with an embossing stylus. Press firmly, but not so hard that you penetrate the foil. When finished, emboss the second and third sheets of foil.

4 Heat all three copper pieces with a butane torch, which causes the metal to change color. Dip the copper in a bowl of water periodically to cool it, and then reheat as necessary to obtain the desired colors. Allow the copper to cool completely.

5 Apply black metallic rub-ons (the artist recommends using Rub-n-Buff) or acrylic paint over the embossed surface of the copper foil, polishing off the excess with a rag.

6 Turn the copper pieces over (embossed side down), and place a mirror in the center of each. Miter the corners of the square pieces by trimming with scissors. For the circular mirror, cut slits in the copper to ease folding.

7 Place two wire lengths from step 1 between the copper foil and the mirror on each piece, allowing the loops to extend beyond the corners (beyond the edges for the circular piece) as shown. Fold each side of the copper foil over the edges of the mirrors.

8 Apply copper foil tape to the edges of the folded copper pieces, covering the raw copper edges. Buff the surface with a rag.

9 Cut three short lengths of copper wire, and insert three beads on each. Make loops at the ends of each wire with pliers to make connectors. Attach a connector between each copper piece as shown, and use chain-nose pliers to attach a small clasp.

Charmed, I'm Sure

ABSTRACT PAINTING AND STAMPING TECHNIQUES ARE A NEW APPROACH TO ART WITH SHRINK PLASTIC.

This collaborative project combines the skills of painter/stamp artist Sherrill Kahn with my silver- and copper-wire techniques. Sherrill takes a new approach to painting and stamping shrink plastic. Instead of stamping an image, cutting it out around the perimeter, and creating a charm, she stamps and applies paint randomly over an entire sheet of shrink plastic. This creates an abstract painting with pattern stamps and sponged-on paint in brilliant colors. Once both sides of the plastic have been covered with paint, she cuts out her shapes, punches holes in them, and shrinks them. The resulting charms can then be enhanced with more painting and stamping before they are assembled into finished jewelry. I use sterling silver and/or copper wire to incorporate the charms into jewelry.

GETTING STARTED

• *For detailed information on the processes used in making these pieces, consult the sections on Getting Started with Jewelry-Making (page 8), Rubber Stamp Embellishments (page 30) and Shrink Plastic Embellishments (page 45).*

• *This project is completed in two parts: Create several shrink art charms first, and then assemble the charms into jewelry enhanced with beaded dangles.*

PROJECT BY: Sherrill Kahn, Encino, California, and Sharilyn Miller, Aliso Viejo, California
STAMP COMPANY: Impress Me

SHRINK ART CHARMS

shrink art charms

- shrink plastic: clear, translucent and white
- art stamps
- parchment paper
- cardboard
- sponges
- craft scissors
- 1/8" (0.3cm) hole punch
- acrylic enamel
- metallic pens: silver, copper, etc.
- metallic paint
- glass paint
- embossing tool or toaster oven

1. Sponge background paints onto both sides of an 8" x 10" (20.3cm x 25.4cm) sheet of shrink plastic (see the tips box on page 101 for artists' recommendations). Sponge the color lightly or it will be very dark when you shrink it.

2. Once the plastic is dry, apply the same paints to abstract "pattern" stamps. Stamp the patterns randomly on the plastic. Change paint colors and pattern stamps as you cover the surface with designs. Allow the paint to dry thoroughly.

3. Cut out shapes (squares, circles, triangles, rectangles) from the shrink plastic, keeping shrinkage in mind as you determine the size of each piece. Round the corners to reduce sharp points and edges. Use leftover scraps to cut out smaller shapes.

4. Punch a 1/8" (0.3cm) hole near the edge of each plastic piece. Keep in mind that this hole will shrink with the plastic when exposed to heat.

5. Place the charms on parchment paper, and shrink them using either an embossing tool or a toaster oven. Place another piece of parchment paper attached to cardboard over the surface immediately after shrinking, and press down hard to flatten the piece.

6. Once cooled, add more paint and stamping to the charms as desired.

7. To finish, run a metallic pen around the edges of each charm. Use a silver pen with sterling silver wire, a copper pen with copper wire, etc.

Earrings

1 Wrap 20″ (51cm) of 20-gauge copper wire onto 4″ (10.2cm) of 16-gauge copper wire, or wrap 20″ (51cm) of 24-gauge sterling silver wire onto 4″ (10.2cm) of 16-gauge sterling silver wire. **NOTE**: Wrapping the base wire with finer-gauge wire is optional.

2 Place the end of the 16-gauge wire in the tips of the round-nose pliers, and wrap a spiral as described in Getting Started with Jewelry-Making (page 14). Use your fingers to shape the spiral. If using wrapped wire, push the coiled wire down as near to the end of the 16-gauge wire as possible before bending the spiral.

3 To finish the spiral, grasp the tip of the wire in the middle of the round-nose pliers, and roll it back to create a teardrop.

4 "Dome" the spiral by holding it with the tips of your fingers and gently pushing up the center with the chain-nose pliers.

5 Place a small dot of jewelry adhesive inside the cup of the dome, and affix either an earring hook or clip-on earring back. Allow to dry for 24 hours.

6 Attach an 18-gauge jump ring to the teardrop on the earring spiral and add a small bead if desired. For instructions, refer to Getting Started with Jewelry-Making (page 20). Run the jump ring through one of the shrink art charms. Dangle a smaller shrink art charm from the jump ring if desired.

Bracelet

1 Create six S-links from 16-gauge wire, and create several jump rings from 18-gauge. For S-link instructions, refer to page 25. For jump ring instructions, refer to page 12. The jump rings will be used to connect the S-links and to attach bead dangles and shrink-art charms.

2 To create bead dangles, flush cut several pieces of 18-gauge wire (silver or copper) to 4″ (10.2cm) lengths, and make a tiny spiral at one end of each. String two to four beads onto the wire. About ¾″ (1.9cm) from the last bead, grasp the wire with the back of the round-nose pliers and create a double eye pin, also described in Getting Started with Jewelry-Making (page 18). Wrap down the neck, and bevel-cut the end of the wire. File off any burrs.

3 To assemble the bracelet, connect the S-links with double jump rings to create a long chain. Do not make a circle of the chain yet.

4 The S-link is ideal for making charm bracelets. It provides several points from which to dangle shrink art charms and bead dangles. Start by attaching the largest charms first. Add smaller charms and beads as desired, attaching them with jump rings.

5 Leave one S-link free of bead dangles. It will be used as a clasp, as shown to the right. Connect the S-links from each end to fasten the bracelet.

earrings

- stamped and painted shrink art charms
- small beads
- earring posts or clip-ons
- copper wire (16- and 20-gauge)
- sterling silver wire (16-, 18- and 24-gauge)
- flush cutters
- chain-nose pliers
- round-nose pliers
- jewelry adhesive

bracelet

- stamped and painted shrink art charms
- small- to medium-size beads
- copper wire (16- and 18-gauge)
- sterling silver wire (16- and 18-gauge)
- flush cutters
- flat-nose pliers
- chain-nose pliers
- round-nose pliers
- extra-long round-nose pliers
- hard-plastic mallet
  - chasing hammer
  - steel bench block

NECKLACE

1 Create eight S-links and eight connection links from 16-gauge wire (silver or copper) as described in Getting Started with Jewelry-Making (page 25). Create several 18-gauge wire (silver or copper) jump rings. These will be used to connect the S-links and to attach bead dangles and shrink art charms.

2 To create bead dangles, flush cut several pieces of 18-gauge wire (silver or copper) to 4″ (10.2cm) lengths, and make a tiny spiral at one end of each. String two to four beads onto the wire. About ¾″ (1.9cm) from the last bead, grasp the wire with the back of the round-nose pliers and create a double eye pin, also described in Getting Started with Jewelry-Making (page 18). Wrap down the neck, and bevel-cut the end of the wire. File off any burrs.

3 To assemble the necklace, connect the S-links with double jump rings to create a long chain. Attach four connection links to each end of the chain.

4 Attach shrink art charms to the necklace with jump rings, starting with the largest charms in the center and working outward with progressively smaller charms. Add bead dangles as desired.

5 Create the clasp of your choice and attach it to the necklace.

necklace

- stamped and painted shrink art charms
- small- to medium-size beads
- copper wire (16- and 18-gauge)
- sterling silver wire (16- and 18-gauge)
- flush cutters
- jeweler's file
- chain-nose pliers
- round-nose pliers
- flat-nose pliers
- extra-long round-nose pliers
- hard-plastic mallet
- chasing hammer
- steel bench block

TIPS

- *Any paint that can be used for glazed ceramic tiles, glass or metal can be used on the shrink plastic without sanding. The artist suggests using the following paints: Delta's PermEnamel for opaque effects, although they do have translucent paint as well; Delta's Glass Paint for translucent effects; Pebeo's Vitrea and Porcelaine for translucent effects; DecoArt's Metal Paint or Ultra Gloss for opaque effects; Ranger's Décor-it for great metallics and opaque effects (fantastic for decorating the piece after it has been shrunk); and Jacquard's Pinata Colors.*

- *Both the necklace and bracelet may be lengthened or shortened by adding or subtracting S-link and connection links.*

- *Try making a charm bracelet or necklace with different links, or even with jump rings. To save time, jump rings of various sizes may be purchased in most bead stores.*

PROJECT BY: Gaylynn Stringham, Victorville, California
STAMP COMPANIES: PSX Design; Stampington & Company

BUDDHA'S DELIGHT

A FLAT GLASS MARBLE ADDS DIMENSION TO RUBBER STAMPING.

Placing a flat glass marble over rubber stamped imagery adds instant dimension to the artwork, making this technique ideally suited for jewelry-making. The artist also uses large shards of sea glass—the edges have been softened by years of rolling in the sandy surf—and mounts them all together with strong jewelry adhesive. This layering process opens up a world of possibilities for the stamp artist!

GETTING STARTED

• For detailed information on the processes used in making these pieces, consult the sections on Getting Started in Jewelry-Making (page 8) and Rubber Stamp Embellishments (page 30).

PENDANT

pendant

- art stamp: Buddha
- Chinese coin
- beads
- matboard
- cardstock
- gold foil tape
- necklace chain
- brads
- 26-gauge gold wire
- chain-nose pliers
- round-nose pliers
- craft scissors
- hole punch
- acetate
- permanent inkpad: black
- pigment ink: ochre and rose
- Crafter's ink: turquoise
- colored pencils
- dimensional adhesive
- jewelry adhesive
- embossing tool

1 Stamp the Buddha image on cardstock. Color the image background with ochre and rose-colored pigment ink, and add details with colored pencils.

2 Cut out a 1½″ x 2″ (3.8cm x 5.1cm) rectangle from the stamped image, and adhere it to a piece of matboard cut to the same size. Once the glue has dried, trim the edges as needed.

3 Cut out a piece of 1½″ x 2″ (3.8cm x 5.1cm) window plastic or acetate and place it on top of the stamped image. Secure the layers from steps 1 and 2 with gold foil tape.

4 Punch two holes near the top of the piece and one at the center-bottom. Apply brads to these holes to make jump rings.

5 Apply a dimensional adhesive (the artist recommends using Diamond Glaze) to the foil tape, and dip the piece in small glass beads to adhere them around the edges. Set aside to dry for several hours.

6 Rub a large Chinese coin with turquoise Crafter's ink, and heat-set it with an embossing tool.

7 Make two bead dangles with three beads each, forming the loops with round-nose pliers. Wrap the Chinese coin with wire, adding small beads to the wire as you wrap it on the front side. Add the two bead dangles to the center of three wraps as shown. Create a twisted-wire loop at the top of the coin, first running the wire through the small hole at the center-bottom of the piece from step 4.

8 Attach a commercial or handmade necklace chain with jump rings. For instructions, refer to Getting Started with Jewelry-Making (page 12).

TIP

You might find it easier to use a jump ring to secure the large Chinese coin to the pendant, rather than making a loop that goes through the hole in the pendant.

brooch

- art stamps: Buddha and oriental orchid
- Chinese coin
- sea glass
- beads
- cardstock
- gold foil tape
- flat glass marble
- pin-back
- 26-gauge wire
- chain-nose pliers
- round-nose pliers
- craft scissors
- permanent inkpad: black
- pigment ink: gold, ochre and rose
- crafter's ink: turquoise
- colored pencils
- embossing powder
- gold leafing pen
- dimensional adhesive
- jewelry adhesive
- embossing tool

BROOCH

1 Stamp the Buddha image on cardstock. Color the image background with ochre and rose-colored pigment ink, and add details with colored pencils.

2 Place a large, clear, flat glass marble on the head portion of the image and trace around it lightly. Cut out the image. Spread a layer of dimensional adhesive (the artist recommends using Diamond Glaze) on the back of the marble, and place it on the stamped image. Wrap the edges with gold foil tape, and apply a layer of dimensional adhesive to the foil. Dip the piece in small beads to adhere them and allow to dry.

3 Stamp the Oriental orchid image on a large piece of terra cotta sea glass with gold pigment ink. Emboss it, and apply a gold leafing pen to the edges.

4 Make six small bead dangles with fine-gauge gold wire and three small beads each. Form loops with round-nose pliers, and use chain-nose pliers to attach two dangles together as shown, forming three double-dangles. For instructions, refer to Getting Started with Jewelry-Making (page 24).

5 Use jewelry adhesive (the artist recommends using E6000) to adhere the marble from step 2 to the top of the stamped sea glass. Adhere the bead dangles to the bottom of the sea glass, and glue a smaller piece of sea glass on top of the wires.

6 Rub a small Chinese coin with turquoise Crafter's ink, and heat-set it with an embossing tool. Adhere it to the small piece of sea glass from step 4.

7 Adhere a pin-back to the back of the brooch with jewelry adhesive and allow to dry for 24 hours before wearing.

ALL WRAPPED UP
TUBULAR FUN WITH POLYMER CLAY AND STAMPS.

Your clay beads don't have to be perfectly stamped and shaped to make nice jewelry pieces. The rough, textured edges of MariaTeresa Stoa's brooch, earrings and necklace add to the overall effect of her ethnically inspired set. The copper-colored rollup beads act as tubes which are held in place with jewel-toned yarns and fibers. The artist sets a mood that is further enhanced by the application of metallic paints and powders.

GETTING STARTED

• *For detailed information on the processes used in making this project, consult the sections on Rubber Stamp Embellishments (page 8), Polymer Clay Embellishments (page 33) and Fiber Art Embellishments (page 41) .*
• *Prepare and condition polymer clay, mixing a small portion of translucent clay with copper-colored clay.*

necklace

- polymer clay: translucent and copper
- two crimp beads, one for each side of clasp
- art stamps
- beads
- assorted fibers and yarns
- toggle clasp
- copper wire, 24-gauge
- bead stringing wire, 36"
- round-nose pliers
- needle-nose pliers
- gold leaf
- powdered pigments
- glitter spray
- metallic paints
- permanent inkpad: black
- jewelry adhesive
- toaster oven
- rolling pin or hand-cranked pasta machine

NECKLACE

1 When your clay has been conditioned and mixed well, add bits of gold leaf by hand or by running the clay through a hand-cranked pasta machine.

2 Roll out the clay to ⅛" (0.3cm) thick.

3 Stamp various images randomly into the surface of the clay. When you've covered the surface with impressions, gently tear the clay into small and large strips with rough edges.

4 Roll these strips to create small and large rollup beads, making sure the holes are quite large. For this necklace, make two large beads (about 3" [7.6cm] in length) and two small tubes (about 1" [2.5cm] in length).

5 Bake the rollup beads at 275˚F (135˚C) for 25 minutes, taking care not to burn them. Remove them from the oven and allow to cool.

6 Paint the surface of each bead lightly with metallic paints, and apply small amounts of powdered pigments as well (the artist recommends using Lumiere metallic paints and Pearl Ex powdered pigments). Allow the paint to dry completely, and lightly spray the surface with glitter paint.

7 Cut six to eight strands of yarn or fiber 6½" to 8" (16.5cm to 20.3cm) long. Run the yarn and fiber through the large rollup beads and tie knots at each end to secure in place. Double-knot if necessary. Several inches should protrude from each end.

8 Spiral copper wire as described in Getting Started with Jewelry-Making (page 14). Secure the ends to the protruding yarn or fiber. Add beads to the wire and bend it into interesting shapes. Tuck the wire ends into the beads and secure them in place with jewelry adhesive if necessary.

9 To make a necklace, string color-coordinated beads onto bead stringing wire (the artist recommends using Soft Flex or Beadalon). First, thread a crimp bead, then make a loop through the toggle clasp, and finally secure the toggle clasp to one end with the crimp bead.

(CON'T ON NEXT PAGE)

PROJECT BY: MariaTeresa Stoa, Ramah, New Mexico
STAMP COMPANIES: Inkadinkado, Just for Fun, Stampers Anonymous

10 When you've strung about 7½" (19.1cm), add one of the small rollup beads you made with clay. Continue stringing 2" (5.1cm) more beads, and then add one of the large rollup beads festooned with yarn or fibers and wire.

11 Run the beading wire through the large rollup bead, and continue beading about 4" (10.2cm) more. Add another large rollup bead, and continue up the opposite side of the necklace.

12 Add another crimp bead, making a loop through the end of the toggle clasp, and secure the clasp with the crimp bead.

BROOCH

1 When your clay has been conditioned and mixed well, add bits of gold leaf by hand or by running the clay through a hand-cranked pasta machine.

2 Roll out the clay to about ⅛" (0.3cm) thickness.

3 Stamp various images randomly into the surface of the clay. When you've covered the surface with stamped impressions, gently tear the clay into small and large strips with rough edges.

4 Roll up one strip to create a large rollup bead (about 2" [5.1cm] long), making sure the hole is quite large. Tear off another chunk of clay to make the base of the brooch (about 3¼" x 1¼" [8.3cm x 3.2cm]). Shape it as desired, pressing the clay together in the middle to form a funnel shape.

5 Bake the brooch and rollup bead at 275˚F (135˚C) for 25 minutes, taking care not to burn them. Remove the brooch and rollup bead from the oven and allow to cool.

6 Paint the surfaces of the brooch and bead lightly with metallic paints, and apply small amounts of powdered pigments as well (the artist recommends using Lumiere metallic paints and Pearl Ex powdered pigments). Allow the paint to dry completely, and lightly spray the surfaces with glitter paint.

7 Cut six to eight strands of yarn or fiber 12" (30.5cm) in length each, double them over, and tie a knot. Push the knot through the funnel shape in the brooch, created in step 4. Fasten it in place with strong jewelry adhesive (the artist recommends using E6000).

8 Spiral the copper wire as described in Getting Started with Jewelry-Making (page 14) and secure the ends to the protruding yarns above and below the funnel shape. Add beads to the wire, and bend it into interesting shapes. Tuck the wire ends into the funnel and secure them in place, using strong jewelry adhesive if necessary.

9 Run a piece of copper wire through the tube bead and create an eye pin at one end. For instructions, see Getting Started with Jewelry-Making (page 18). Attach the eye pin to the spiral protruding from the base brooch. On the opposite end of the rollup bead, string a large bead onto the wire, and secure it in place with another wrapped eye pin. Attach dangling brass charms or beads.

10 Glue a pin-back to the back of the brooch and let dry 24 hours before wearing.

brooch

- polymer clay: translucent and copper
- art stamps
- beads
- assorted fibers and yarns
- pin-back
- copper wire, 24-gauge
- round-nose pliers
- needle-nose pliers
- gold leaf
- powdered pigments
- glitter spray
- metallic paints
- permanent inkpad: black
- jewelry adhesive
- toaster oven
- rolling pin or hand-cranked pasta machine

EARRINGS

1 When your clay has been conditioned and mixed well, add bits of gold leaf by hand or by running the clay through a hand-cranked pasta machine.

2 Roll out the clay to about ⅛″ (0.3cm) thickness.

3 Stamp various images randomly into the surface of the clay. When you've covered the surface with stamped impressions, gently tear the clay into two diamond-shaped pieces about 1½″ x 2″ (3.8cm x 5.1cm), with rough edges.

4 Poke three holes near the bottom of each diamond shape.

5 Bake the pieces at 275˚F (135˚C) for 25 minutes, taking care not to burn them. Remove them from the oven and allow to cool.

6 Paint the surfaces lightly with metallic paints, and apply small amounts of powdered pigments as well (the artist recommends using Lumiere metallic paints and Pearl Ex powdered pigments). Allow the paint to dry completely, and then lightly spray the surfaces with glitter paint.

7 Make bead dangles with wire jump rings, beads and charms as described in Getting Started with Jewelry-Making (page 12). Attach them to the holes near the bottom of each clay piece.

8 Spiral some copper wire and run it through a face bead. For instructions, refer to Getting Started with Jewelry-Making (page 14). Affix it to the front of each clay piece with strong jewelry adhesive (the artist recommends using E6000).

9 Cut several strands of yarn and fiber to about 5″ (12.7cm) long, and affix them to the back of each clay piece with a strong jewelry adhesive. Glue post or clip-on earring findings to the back as well, on top of the fibers. Allow the glue to dry for 24 hours before wearing your earrings.

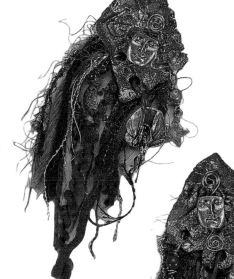

TIPS

• The brooch easily converts into a necklace pendant by affixing a necklace bail to the back instead of a pin-back.

• Instead of stringing your necklace with beads, try using small found objects like coins, game pieces or items from the hardware store. Or make your own beads with scrap polymer clay.

HEART & HAND

PUT HEART INTO YOUR ART...AND REAP THE BENEFITS.

K ori Pilney has a distinctive, whimsical style with rubber stamps. She used purple elastic for the bracelet band and red ball-chain to make a necklace with images of hearts, hands, stripes, checks and spirals. This artist is very bold in her color choices, and the combination of folk-style stamp images with the warmest colors in the spectrum give energy and life to this jewelry set.

GETTING STARTED

•For *detailed information on the processes used in making this project, consult the sections on Rubber Stamp Embellishments (page 30), Polymer Clay Embellishments (page 33) and Shrink Plastic Embellishments (page 45).*

*enlarge template
200%, then 125%*

PROJECT BY: Kori Pilney, San Diego, California
STAMP COMPANIES: All Night Media, A Stamp in the Hand, Hero Arts, Judi-Kins, Magenta, Paula Best Designs, Rubber Stampede, Stampa Rosa

necklace

•shrink plastic: clear
•polymer clay
•art stamps
•brass charms (hands)
•tube bead, 1¼″ long
•ball-chain: red
•craft scissors
•hole punch
•watercolor crayons
 embossing powder
•permanent inkpad: black
•jewelry adhesive
•toaster oven
•hand-cranked pasta
 machine or rolling pin

NECKLACE

1 Color the clear shrink plastic with watercolor crayons (the artist recommends using Caran D'Ache watercolor crayons).

2 Stamp heart, star and hand images onto the plastic with black permanent ink. Stamp each image repeatedly to make lots of charms for the necklace and a face image for the doll pendant. Cut out the images.

3 Punch a hole near the top of each charm to attach to the ball-chain necklace later.

4 Shrink the plastic pieces in a 300°F (149°C) oven for six minutes or until flat. Immediately dip the heated, shrunken plastic pieces in clear embossing powder (the artist recommends using Amazing Glaze), and return them to the oven for two to five minutes.

5 Remove the pieces from the oven, allow them to cool, and adhere them with strong jewelry adhesive (the artist recommends using E6000). Reserve the face image for the doll pendant.

6 Roll out conditioned polymer clay on the #3 setting on a hand-cranked pasta machine (the artist recommends using an Atlas Pasta Machine). Use the template provided to cut out a doll's body. Stamp into the clay body with various images, using black permanent ink.

7 Roll polymer clay snakes for arms, pinch them at the shoulders, and insert brass hands at the wrists. Bake the body and arms at 275°F (135°C) for 25 minutes, taking care not to burn the clay. Remove them from the oven and allow to cool. If necessary, glue the brass hands into the wrists.

8 Adhere the doll body to the arms with strong jewelry adhesive. Adhere the shrink art charms from steps 1 to 5, including several small stars and the face image. Adhere a 1¼″ (3.2cm) long tube bead to the back of the doll pendant with jewelry adhesive. Allow the ensemble to dry for 24 hours.

9 Run the red ball-chain through the shrink art charms. Use a small dab of jewelry adhesive to glue each one in place so that they don't move up and down the chain.

10 Run the ball-chain through the large tube bead.

Bracelet

1 Stamp images onto prepared polymer clay using black permanent ink. Cut out stamped clay pieces in circles, squares, triangles and other shapes. Cut additional pieces of clay in graduated sizes. Punch or poke small holes in each clay piece in order to adhere them to the bracelet.

2 Bake the clay pieces at 275˚F (135˚C) for 25 minutes, taking care not to burn the clay. Remove the baked pieces from the oven and allow to cool.

3 Color the clear shrink plastic with watercolor crayons (the artist recommends using Caran D'Ache watercolor crayons).

4 Stamp various images onto the plastic with black permanent ink. Stamp each image three or four times to make enough charms for the bracelet. Cut out the images. Punch small holes in each piece near the top.

5 Shrink the plastic pieces in a 300˚F (149˚C) oven for six minutes or until flat. Immediately dip heated, shrunken plastic pieces in clear embossing powder (the artist recommends using Amazing Glaze), and return them to the oven for two to five minutes.

6 Remove the pieces from the oven and allow to cool.

7 Cut a piece of elastic to fit your wrist.

8 Use beading thread and a needle to attach the shrink art charms to the elastic. Add beads as desired, and layer shrink art charms as shown. Use strong jewelry adhesive (the artist recommends using E6000) to layer the polymer clay pieces from steps 1 and 2. Sew them to the bracelet.

9 Sew the elastic together, and attach a large polymer clay piece to the seam with beading thread.

TIPS

• *Since a lot of glue is used in this project, it is important to use a strong, clear-drying adhesive. Apply it sparingly and wipe off any excess immediately with a damp cloth.*

• *Ball-chain is widely available at many craft stores, but it can be substituted with a handmade metal chain or other materials of your choice.*

bracelet
- shrink plastic: clear
- polymer clay
- art stamps
- beads
- elastic
- beading thread
- beading needle
- craft scissors
- hole punch
- embossing powder
- permanent inkpad: black
- watercolor crayons
- jewelry adhesive
- toaster oven
- hand-cranked pasta machine or rolling pin

EARRINGS

1 Color the clear shrink plastic with watercolor crayons (the artist recommends using Caran D'Ache watercolor crayons).

2 Stamp heart, star and hand images onto the plastic with black permanent ink. Stamp each image at least twice to make duplicates for earrings.

3 Cut out the images, including four stars, two hearts with hands, and two hearts with stars.

4 Shrink the plastic pieces in a 300°F (149°C) oven for about six minutes or until flat. Immediately dip the heated, shrunken plastic pieces in clear embossing powder (the artist recommends using Amazing Glaze), and return them to the oven for two to five minutes.

5 Remove the pieces from the oven, allow them to cool, and adhere them with strong jewelry adhesive (the artist recommends using E6000).

6 Affix post or clip-on earring backs to the back of each earring with jewelry adhesive. Allow to dry for 24 hours before wearing.

BROOCH

1 Stamp an image onto prepared polymer clay using black permanent ink. Cut out clay circles in graduated sizes.

2 Bake the clay pieces at 275°F (135°C) for 25 minutes, taking care not to burn the clay. Remove the baked pieces from the oven and allow to cool.

3 Affix the circles as shown with jewelry adhesive (the artist recommends using E6000). Allow the pieces to dry, forming a base for the brooch, and then drill a small hole through all the layers.

4 Color the clear shrink plastic with watercolor crayons (the artist recommends using Caran D'Ache watercolor crayons). Stamp various images onto the plastic with black permanent ink. Cut out the images. Punch small holes in each piece near the top.

5 Shrink the plastic pieces in a 300°F (135°C) oven for six minutes or until flat. Immediately dip the heated, shrunken plastic pieces in clear embossing powder (the artist recommends using Amazing Glaze), and return them to the oven for two to five minutes.

6 Remove the pieces from the oven and allow to cool.

7 Run beading thread through the holes in the shrink art charms with a beading needle, adding small beads as desired. Then, run thread through the hole in the polymer clay piece made in step 3. Secure the thread, and tie a good knot to hold the shrink art pieces to the clay brooch.

8 Affix a pin-back to the brooch with jewelry adhesive and allow to dry for 24 hours before wearing.

earrings

·shrink plastic: clear
·art stamps
·earring backs
·craft scissors
·embossing powder
·permanent inkpad: black
·watercolor crayons
·jewelry adhesive
·toaster oven

brooch

·shrink plastic: clear
·polymer clay
·art stamps
·beads
·beading thread
·beading needle
·pin-back
·hole punch
·craft scissors
·embossing powder
·permanent inkpad: black
·watercolor crayons
·toaster oven
·hand-cranked pasta machine or rolling pin
·small drill

GILDED GINKGOS

USE A GINKGO-PATTERNED STAMP TO SHAPE EXOTIC JEWELRY.

This lovely set makes use of a clay mold created from a commercial rubber stamp. The mold is the "negative" into which more clay is pressed to recreate the positive image. The shapes for the jewelry are formed, baked and sanded to a smooth matte surface. Then, the pieces are embellished with the pattern and accented with a gold-leaf pen.

GETTING STARTED

•*For detailed information on the processes used in making this project, consult the sections on Getting Started with Jewelry-Making (page 8), Rubber Stamp Embellishments (page 30) and Polymer Clay Embellishments (page 33).*

PROJECT BY: Patricia Kimle, Ames, Iowa
STAMP COMPANY: Stamp Zia

create a mold

- •polymer clay
- •unmounted art stamp
- •craft knife
- •cornstarch baby powder (not talc)
- •toaster oven
- •hand-cranked pasta machine or rolling pin

pendant

- •polymer clay: navy, ecru and taupe
- •liquid polymer clay
- •320-, 400- and 600-grit wet-dry sandpaper
- •accent beads
- •bead mold (see above)
- •gold chain
- •6″ (15.2cm) 18-gauge gold wire
- •pliers
- •craft scissors
- •tissue blade
- •cornstarch baby powder (not talc)
- •gold leafing pen
- •cyanoacrylate glue
- •toaster oven
- •hand-cranked pasta machine or rolling pin
- •small drill

CREATE A MOLD

1 Roll out a consistent sheet of clay to medium (approximately 1mm) thickness on a hand-cranked pasta machine.

2 Cut out a piece of clay the same size as the ginkgo art stamp.

NOTE: The stamp you will use for this technique must be unmounted. Apply powder to the clay to eliminate all tackiness; the surface should feel dry to the touch.

3 Reset the pasta machine to its widest setting (approximately 3mm), and roll the clay and the stamp through together.

4 Carefully separate the unmounted stamp from the clay. Trim the clay sheet around the pattern. Bake the clay according to the package directions and allow to cool.

PENDANT

1 Photocopy and cut out paper templates for the pendant and raised decoration. Condition the navy clay, and use the base pendant template to form the pendant, making it about ³⁄₈″ (1cm) thick. It should be tapered on all edges and smoothed as much as possible.

2 Bake the clay pendant and allow to cool. Wet-sand it with 320-, then 400- and finally 600-grit wet-dry sandpaper. Set aside.

3 Mix some of the navy clay with ecru and taupe clay to create marbled sheets. Roll out the sheets to a medium (1mm) thickness. Powder the clay.

(CON'T ON NEXT PAGE)

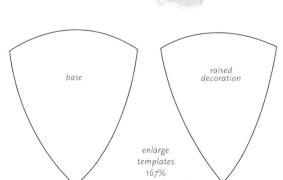

base

raised decoration

enlarge templates 167%

4 Reset the pasta machine to its widest setting (approximately 3mm), and roll the clay and the ginkgo mold through together.

5 Using the raised decoration template, cut out two shapes—one for the front and one for the back of the pendant.

6 Paint a thin layer of liquid polymer clay (the artist recommends using Liquid Sculpey) on the back of each marbled piece. Press both pieces onto the navy base pendant, taking care not to smash the raised pattern. Re-bake and allow to cool.

7 Paint all the raised lines on the decoration with a gold leafing pen.

8 Using a hand drill and 1mm bit, drill holes at the top of the pendant.

9 Using 18-gauge gold wire, form eye pins as described in Getting Started with Jewelry-Making (page 18). Add accent beads and glue the eye pins into the pendant using cyanoacrylate glue. Connect the gold chain.

bracelet

- polymer clay: navy, ecru and taupe
- liquid polymer clay
- bead mold
- cardboard tube or small can
- 320-, 400- and 600-grit wet-dry sandpaper
- gold leafing pen
- cornstarch baby powder (not talc)
- toaster oven
- hand-cranked pasta machine or rolling pin

BRACELET

1 Photocopy and cut out paper templates for the bracelet and the raised decoration to the right. Try the bracelet template on your wrist, and make pattern adjustments as needed to fit.

2 Roll out a thick piece of conditioned navy clay. Using the bracelet template, cut out the bracelet shape. Taper the ends in width and thickness, and form it around a cardboard tube or small can to support the wide center.

3 Bake the bracelet and allow to cool. Wet-sand it with 320-, then 400- and finally 600-grit wet-dry sandpaper. Set aside.

4 Mix some of the navy clay with ecru and taupe clay to create marbled sheets. Roll out the sheets to a medium (1mm) thickness. Powder the clay.

5 Reset the pasta machine to its widest setting (approximately 3mm) and roll the clay and the ginkgo mold through together.

6 Using the raised decoration template, cut out a shape for the top of the bracelet.

7 Paint a thin layer of liquid polymer clay (the artist recommends using Liquid Sculpey) on the back of the marbled piece. Press it onto the bracelet base, taking care not to smash the raised pattern. Re-bake the bracelet and allow to cool.

8 Paint all the raised lines with the gold leafing pen.

raised decoration

base

enlarge templates 200%

Earrings

earrings

- polymer clay: navy, ecru and taupe
- liquid polymer clay
- accent beads
- bead mold (see page 113)
- 320-, 400- and 600-grit sandpaper
- earring hooks: gold
- 6" of 18-gauge gold wire
- pliers
- gold leafing pen
- cornstarch baby powder (not talc)
- cyanoacrylate glue
- toaster oven
- hand-cranked pasta machine or rolling pin
- small drill

1 Photocopy and cut out paper templates for the earrings and raised decorations. Condition the navy clay, and use the earring template below to form the earrings, making them about ³/₈" (1cm) thick. It should be tapered on all edges, and smoothed as much as possible.

2 Bake the earrings and allow to cool. Wet-sand it with 320-, then 400- and finally 600-grit wet-dry sandpaper. Set aside.

3 Mix some of the navy clay with ecru and taupe clay to create marbled sheets. Roll out the sheets to a medium (1mm) thickness. Powder the clay sheet.

4 Reset the pasta machine to its widest setting (approximately 3mm) and roll the clay and the ginkgo mold through together.

5 Using the earring template, cut out four raised decorations for the earrings (two each, front and back).

6 Paint a thin layer of liquid polymer clay (the artist recommends using Liquid Sculpey) on the back of each marbled piece. Press one onto each side of the base earring pendants, taking care not to smash the raised pattern. Re-bake and allow to cool.

7 Paint all the raised lines with the gold leafing pen.

8 Using a drill and 1mm bit, drill holes at the top of each earring pendant.

9 Using 18-gauge gold wire, form eye pins for each earring. For instructions, refer to Getting Started with Jewelry-Making (page 18). Add accent beads, and glue the eye pins into the earring pendants using cyanoacrylate glue. Connect the gold earring hooks.

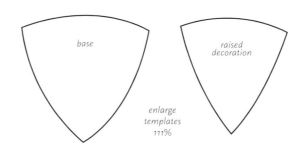

base

raised decoration

enlarge templates 111%

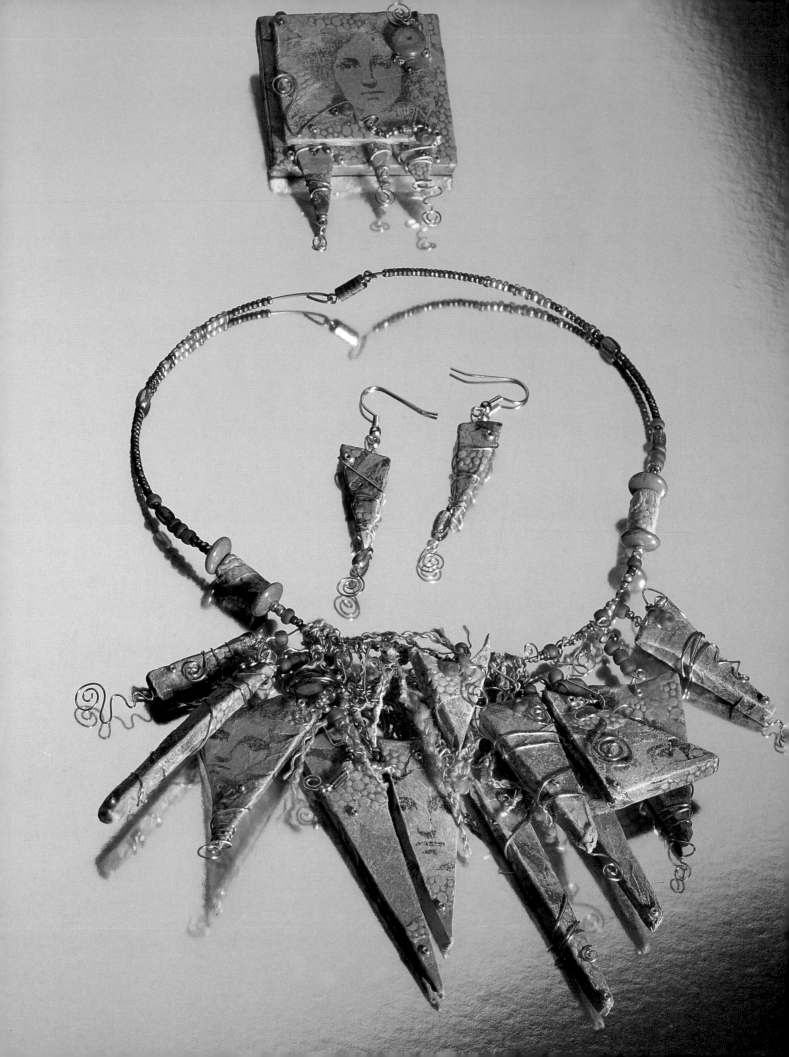

HER FACE

TINY COLLAGED PIECES WRAPPED WITH WIRE MAKE UP THIS UNUSUAL JEWELRY SET.

An enigmatic face peers out of the pastel jungle created by soft textured papers, gold wire and delicate beads. This is the basis for a jewelry set made from foamcore board. This common material, used by artists for a wide variety of purposes, has become one of Diana Twedt's favorite materials for lightweight jewelry sets like this one. The odds and ends from a larger project inspired this serendipitous creation.

GETTING STARTED

•*For detailed information on the processes used in making this project, consult the sections on Getting Started with Jewelry-Making (page 8) and Rubber Stamp Embellishments (page 30).*

earrings
- foamcore board
- textured paper
- art stamp
- decoupage medium
- tissue paper
- beads
- earring hooks
- 26-gauge gold wire
- craft scissors
- paintbrush
- archival inkpad: black
- acrylic paint: ivory and gold
- clear-drying glue
- jewelry adhesive

EARRINGS

1 Stamp an image repeatedly with black archival ink (the artist recommends Memories archival ink) onto tissue paper. Tear around the stamped images. Set them aside.

2 Cut out two small triangular pieces of foamcore board measuring ½" x 1" (1.3cm x 2.5cm), and set them aside.

3 Tear and/or cut decorative or textured paper into very small pieces. Paper scraps from other art projects are ideal. When you have a small pile of paper prepared, glue the pieces onto both foamcore board pieces in a pleasing arrangement. Add the stamped tissue paper as well. Seal both pieces with decoupage medium and allow to dry.

4 Drybrush the surfaces very lightly with gold and ivory acrylic paints.

5 Wrap both triangular pieces with 26-gauge gold wire, and spiral the ends as described in Getting Started with Jewelry-Making (page 14). Add seed beads or decorative beads to the wire as desired.

6 Make two small loops of 26-gauge gold wire, and pierce the ends into the tops of the foamcore board triangles. Add a dab of strong jewelry adhesive to secure the wire loops if necessary.

7 Attach commercial or handmade earring hooks to the loops.

PROJECT BY: Diana Twedt, Rudyard, Montana
STAMP COMPANY: Acey Deucy

BROOCH

1 Stamp an image with black archival ink (the artist recommends using Memories ink) onto tissue paper. Tear around the stamped image until your tissue piece is about 1" (2.5cm) square. Set aside.

2 Cut foamcore board into two pieces, one measuring 1¾" (4.5cm) square, the other measuring 2" (5.1cm) square. Cut out three small triangles of foamcore board.

3 Tear and/or cut textured paper into small, manageable pieces. Paper scraps from other art projects are perfect for this small piece. When you have a small pile of paper prepared, glue the pieces onto both square foamcore board pieces in a pleasing arrangement. Adhere the stamped tissue paper to the front of the smaller foamcore board piece. Seal both pieces with decoupage medium and allow to dry.

4 Drybrush the surfaces very lightly with gold and ivory acrylic paints.

5 Glue the smaller square board to the center of the larger board.

6 Wrap the three small triangular pieces with 26-gauge gold wire, and spiral the ends as described in Getting Started with Jewelry-Making (page 14). Affix the small triangular pieces to the brooch as shown.

7 Shape 26-gauge gold wire into small spirals, and add a few seed beads. Affix the wire to the top of the brooch with jewelry adhesive. Affix seed beads and larger decorative beads as well. Allow the brooch to dry.

8 Affix a pin-back with jewelry adhesive and allow to dry for 24 hours before wearing.

brooch

- foamcore board
- textured paper
- art stamp
- decoupage medium
- tissue paper
- beads
- pin-back
- 26-gauge gold wire
- craft scissors
- paintbrush
- archival inkpad: black
- acrylic paint: ivory and gold
- clear-drying glue
- jewelry adhesive

TIP

This project perfectly illustrates the old maxim, "Collage artists never throw anything away." Diana Twedt saves all her foamcore board scraps from other art projects, and uses them to make jewelry pieces. The pieces can be cut and shaped to preferred specifications.

NECKLACE

1 Stamp an image repeatedly with black archival ink (the artist recommends using Memories ink) onto tissue paper. Tear around the stamped images. Set them aside.

2 Cut out several small triangular pieces of foamcore board and set them aside.

3 Tear and/or cut decorative or textured paper into very small pieces. Paper scraps from other art projects are ideal. When you have a small pile of paper prepared, glue the pieces onto the triangular foamcore board pieces in a pleasing arrangement. Add the stamped tissue paper as well. Seal all pieces with decoupage medium and allow to dry.

4 Drybrush the surfaces very lightly with gold and ivory acrylic paints.

5 Wrap the triangular pieces with 26-gauge gold wire, and spiral the ends as described in Getting Started with Jewelry-Making (page 14). Add seed beads or decorative beads to the wire as desired.

6 Make small loops of 26-gauge gold wire, and pierce the ends into the tops of the foamcore board triangles. Add a dab of strong jewelry adhesive to secure the wire loops if necessary.

7 Cut a piece of 18-gauge silver wire to about 16″ (40.6cm) long, creating a choker-length neck wire. Attach the foamcore board triangles to the wire by creating jump rings as described in Getting Started with Jewelry-Making (page 12). Or, make small bead dangles, attaching one end of each dangle to the neck wire and the other end to a triangular piece. For instructions, refer to Getting Started with Jewelry-Making (page 15). Add small seed beads between each triangular piece as shown.

8 When all the triangular pieces are attached, add a few strands of color-coordinating fibers. Then, add seed beads and larger decorative beads to the neck wire as shown.

9 Turn over each end of the neck wire to create loops that hold a commercial or handmade clasp. This will keep the beads from slipping off the wire.

necklace

- foamcore board
- textured paper
- art stamp
- decoupage medium
- tissue paper
- beads
- fibers
- clasp
- 26-gauge gold wire
- 18-gauge silver wire
- chain-nose pliers
- round-nose pliers
- craft scissors
- paintbrush
- archival inkpad: black
- acrylic paint: ivory and gold
- clear-drying glue
- jewelry adhesive

DOMINO ADORNMENTS

POPULAR GAME PIECES MAKE GREAT STAMPING SURFACES.

This project proves that stamping can be done on just about any surface—even domino game pieces. By using permanent heat-set inks to color her dominoes and stamp intriguing images, Tara Ross multiplies the possibilities for jewelry-making with rubber stamps. Stamped and colored dominoes may be drilled, glued, wire-wrapped and otherwise manipulated in countless ways to make pretty pendants, dangle earrings or contemporary brooches.

GETTING STARTED

•*For detailed information on the processes used in making this project, consult the sections on Getting Started with Jewelry-Making (page 8) and Rubber Stamp Embellishments (page 30).*

PROJECT BY: Tara Ross, Shoreline, Washington
STAMP COMPANY: Art Chix Studio

pendant

•large (2″ x 1″ [5.1cm x 2.5cm]) domino
•matchbox
•art stamp
•ball-chain
•¹⁄₂″ (1.3cm) copper tubing
•¹⁄₄″ (0.6cm) copper tubing
•tubing cutter
•sponge
•permanent heat-set ink: black and additional colors as desired
•acrylic paint: ivory and copper
•jewelry adhesive
•embossing tool

PENDANT

1 Sponge permanent heat-set ink (the artist recommends using Ancient Page) in the color of your choice onto the back of a large domino, and heat-set with an embossing tool. Add more ink as desired, and heat-set when finished.

2 Stamp images in black permanent ink and heat-set. Set aside.

3 Paint the outside of a matchbox with ivory acrylic paint and the inside drawer with copper acrylic paint. Allow it to dry.

4 Stamp the matchbox using black permanent ink.

5 Cut two 1″ (2.5cm) long pieces of ¹⁄₄″ (0.6cm) copper tubing and one 1¹⁄₂″ (3.8cm) piece of ¹⁄₂″ (1.3cm) copper tubing with a tubing cutter. Adhere the large tubing piece to the bottom of the matchbox and the small tubing pieces to each side of the matchbox as shown, using jewelry adhesive. Allow to dry for 24 hours.

6 Run the ball-chain through the copper tubing to make a necklace.

earrings

•2 small (1¹⁄₄″ x ¹⁄₂″ [3.2cm x 1.3cm]) dominoes
•art stamp
•earring hooks
•silver coiled wire
•sponge
•permanent heat-set ink: black and additional colors as desired
•jewelry adhesive
•embossing (heat) tool

EARRINGS

1 Sponge permanent heat-set ink (the artist recommends using Ancient Page) in the color of your choice onto the back of two small dominoes, and heat-set with an embossing tool. Add more ink as desired, and heat-set when finished.

2 Stamp images in black permanent ink and heat-set.

3 Cut two lengths of silver coiled wire, each about ¹⁄₂″ (1.3cm) long, and adhere them to the tops of the dominoes with jewelry adhesive. Allow to dry for 24 hours.

4 Attach earring hooks.

JEWELRY BOX

1 Sponge permanent heat-set ink (the artist recommends using Ancient Page) in the color of your choice all over a papier maché book-shaped box, and heat-set with an embossing tool. Repeat sponging inks on a small domino and heat-set.

2 Stamp the box and domino with black permanent heat-set ink and heat-set. Set aside.

3 Coil copper wire into a pleasing shape, and adhere it to the front of the box with jewelry adhesive. For instructions, refer to Getting Started with Jewelry-Making (page 15). Adhere the domino in place over the copper wire. Allow the box to dry for 24 hours, and use it to store your domino earrings.

jewelry box
- small (1¼" x ½" [3.2cm x 1.3cm]) domino
- papier maché book box 2" x 3" x 1" (5.1cm x 1.6cm x 2.5cm)
- art stamp
- copper wire
- sponge
- permanent heat-set ink: black and additional colors as desired
- jewelry adhesive
- embossing tool

BROOCH

1 Sponge permanent heat-set ink (the artist recommends using Ancient Page ink) in the color of your choice onto the back of a small domino, and heat-set with an embossing tool. Add more ink as desired, and heat-set when finished.

2 Stamp an image in black permanent ink and heat-set.

3 Glue the domino to the center of a metal film negative slide with jewelry adhesive.

4 Glue a length of ball-chain around the perimeter of the domino. Adhere three snaps beneath it. Add ½" (1.3cm) of silver coiled wire to the top. For instructions, refer to Getting Started with Jewelry-Making (page 15).

5 Adhere two sewing hooks to the top of the metal film negative slide. Allow to dry for 24 hours.

6 Cut coiled wire about 3" (7.6cm) long, and run each end through the sewing hooks on the brooch.

7 Adhere a pin-back to the brooch and allow to dry for 24 hours before wearing.

brooch
- small (1¼" x ½" [3.2cm x 1.3cm]) domino
- metal film negative slide
- art stamp
- ball-chain
- snaps
- pin-back
- silver coiled wire
- sewing hooks
- sponge
- permanent heat-set ink: black and additional colors as desired
- jewelry adhesive
- embossing tool

necklace

- 3 large (2″ x 1″ [5.1cm x 2.5cm]) dominoes
- art stamp
- crimp beads
- alphabet beads
- waxed linen thread
- clasp
- coiled silver wire
- sewing hooks
- sponge
- permanent heat-set ink: black and additional colors as desired
- jewelry adhesive
- embossing tool

NECKLACE

1 Sponge permanent ink (the artist recommends using Ancient Page) in the color of your choice onto the back of three large dominoes, and heat-set with an embossing tool. Add more ink as desired, and heat-set when finished.

2 Stamp images in black permanent ink and heat-set. Set them aside.

3 Cut three lengths of silver coiled wire ¾″ long each, and adhere to the top of each domino with jewelry adhesive. For instructions, refer to Getting Started with Jewelry-Making (page 15). Add sewing hooks as embellishments. Allow the dominoes to dry for 24 hours.

4 String the dominoes on a length of waxed linen thread, adding alphabet letters between each domino.

5 Attach a clasp with crimp beads.

TIP

Copper tubing is available at many hardware and home-improvement centers. The artist obtained her tubing from an airplane-surplus warehouse. When searching for unique materials for your jewelry, try unusual outlets like electronics stores, thrift shops, auto-parts stores and metal-surplus retailers.

RESOURCES

Your local art supply store, rubber stamp retailer and bead store will provide you with nearly all the materials you need to make beautiful rubber stamped jewelry. Hardware stores and home improvement outlets supply a variety of useful tools and materials as well, including vinyl and copper tubing, tube cutters, metal shears and much more. Check out your local stained glass shop for beveled glass pieces, copper tape and related supplies. If you have difficulty locating needed materials, tool, and supplies in your area, the following resources should be helpful.

Stamp Companies

A STAMP IN THE HAND
www.astampinthehand.com
→ *red rubber and hardwood maple stamps*

ACEY DEUCY
Phone: (518) 398-5108
→ *stamps*

ALL NIGHT MEDIA
www.allnightmedia.com
→ *stamps, craft supplies*

ART CHIX STUDIO
www.artchixstudio.com
→ *stamps, jewelry, fabric, craft supplies*

CLEARSNAP
www.clearsnap.com
→ *inkpads, stamps*

HERO ARTS
www.heroarts.com
→ *stamps, craft supplies*

IMPRESS ME RUBBER STAMPS
www.impressmenow.com
→ *stamps*

INKADINKADO
www.inkadinkado.com
→ *stamps, craft supplies*

JUDI-KINS
www.judikins.com
→ *stamps*

JUST FOR FUN
www.planetrubber.com
→ *stamps, craft supplies*

LASTING IMPRESSIONS
www.lasimppan.com
→ *stamps*

MAGENTA RUBBER STAMPS
www.magentarubberstamps.com
→ *stamps, paper products, craft supplies*

NINA BAGLEY DESIGNS
www.itsmysite.com/ninabagleydesign/
→ *stamps, jewelry, canvases*

ORNAMENTUM
www.cdad.com/orn
→ *stamps*

PAULA BEST DESIGNS
www.paulabest.com
→ *stamps, jewelry*

POSTMODERN DESIGN
postmoderndesign@aol.com
→ *stamps*

PSX DESIGN
www.psxdesign.com
→ *stamps, card-making kits, scrapbooking and craft supplies*

RANGER INDUSTRIES, INC.
www.rangerink.com
→ *embossing tools, inkpads, stamping supplies)*

RENAISSANCE ART STAMPS
P.O. Box 1218
Burlington, CT 06013
→ *stamps*

RUBBER POET
www.rubberpoet.com
→ *stamps*

RUBBER STAMPEDE
www.deltacrafts.com
→ *stamps, craft supplies*

RUBBER STAMP PLANTATION (THE)
www.rsphawaii.com
→ *stamps, stickers, decals, temporary tattoos*

SPEEDBALL
www.speedballart.com
→ *stamp-carving tools and materials*

STAMPERS ANONYMOUS
www.stampersanonymous.com
→ *stamps, stamping supplies*

STAMPING GROUND (THE)
www.stampingground.com
→ *stamps*

STAMPINGTON & COMPANY
www.stampington.com
→ *stamps, stamp accessories, magazines, jewelry*

STAMPOTIQUE ORIGINALS
www.stampotique.com
→ *stamps*

STAMPSMITH (THE)
www.stampsmith.net
→ *stamps*

STAMP ZIA

www.stampzia.com

→ *stamps, stamped memorabilia*

TOYBOX RUBBER STAMPS

www.toyboxart.com

→ *stamps, stamping supplies, inks*

UPTOWN DESIGN COMPANY

www.uptownrubberstamps.com

→ *stamps, stamping supplies*

ZETTIOLOGY

www.thestudiozine.com

→ *stamps, stamped memorabilia*

General Craft Suppliers

AMERICAN TAG COMPANY

www.americantag.com

→ *shipping tags*

CREATIVE PAPERCLAY

www.creativepaperclay.com

→ *paper clay*

DANIEL SMITH , INC.

www.danielsmith.com

→ *art supplies*

DELTA

www.deltacrafts.com

→ *paints, craft supplies*

FISKARS

www.fiskars.com

→ *decorative scissors, craft supplies*

JACQUARD

www.jacquardproducts.com

→ *inks, paints, silk dyes, pigment powders*

KATO POLYCLAY

www.katopolyclay.com

→ *polymer clay tools and supplies*

LUCKY SQUIRREL

www.luckysquirrel.com

→ *shrink plastic*

MARVY-UCHIDA

www.uchida.com

→ *metallic markers*

PEBEO

www.dickblick.com

→ *paints*

PLAID ENTERPRISES, INC.

www.plaidonline.com

→ *paints, craft supplies*

POLYMER CLAY EXPRESS

www.polymerclayexpress.com

→ *polymer clay and related supplies*

RIO GRANDE

www.riogrande.com

→ *jewelry making materials*

SALIS INTERNATIONAL

www.docmartins.com

→ *surface paints*

STAEDTLER

www.staedtler.com

→ *art and craft supplies, stamp-carving block*

THUNDERBIRD SUPPLY

www.thunderbirdsupply.com

→ *jewelry making supplies and tools*

TSUKINEKO

www.tsukineko.com

→ *inkpads*

USARTQUEST, INC.

www.usartquest.com

→ *art and craft supplies*

SUZE WEINBERG

www.schmoozewithsuze.com

→ *art and craft supplies, mixed media, ultra-thick embossing enamel*

INDEX

Create extraordinary art with
Rubber Stamps and more!

  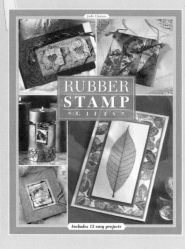 

CREATIVE STAMPING WITH MIXED MEDIA TECHNIQUES • Make your rubber stamp art more colorful, unique and beautiful! Inside you'll find 20 simple recipes that combine sponging, glazing and masking techniques with colorful stamped patterns. Try them out on the 13 step-by-step projects, including a fabric wall hanging, wooden tray, flowerpot, paper lantern, journals, boxes and more. ISBN 1-58180-347-8, PAPERBACK, 128 PAGES, #32315-K

30 MINUTE RUBBER STAMP WORKSHOP • Let Sandra McCall show you how to make gorgeous rubber stamp treasures in 30 minutes or less. From home decor and party favors to desk accessories and wearable gifts, you'll find 27 exciting projects inside. Each one is easy to do and inexpensive to make—perfect for those days when you want to create something quickly! ISBN 1-58180-271-4, PAPERBACK, 128 PAGES, #32142-K

RUBBER STAMP GIFTS • Create rubber stamp masterpieces perfect for gift-giving any time of the year! From jewelry boxes and travel journals to greeting cards and candles, Judy Claxton shows you how to make 12 gorgeous projects using easy-to-find materials and simple techniques, such as embellishing, embossing, direct-to-paper, paper clay, polymer clay and shrink plastic. ISBN 1-58180-466-0, PAPERBACK, 48 PAGES, #32723-K

RUBBER STAMP EXTRAVAGANZA • Use rubber stamps to decorate candles, jewelry, purses, book covers, wall hangings and more. Sixteen step-by-step projects show you how by using creative techniques, surfaces and embellishments, including metal, beads, embossing powder, clay and shrink plastic! ISBN 1-58180-128-9, PAPERBACK, 128 PAGES, #31829-K

These books and other fine North Light titles are available from your local art and craft retailer or bookstore, an online supplier or by calling 1-800-448-0915